MALCOLM HILLIER'S
COLOR GARDEN

MALCOLM HILLIER'S
COLOR GARDEN

Photography by
STEPHEN HAYWARD AND STEVEN WOOSTER

DORLING KINDERSLEY
LONDON • NEW YORK • STUTTGART • MOSCOW

A DORLING KINDERSLEY BOOK

PROJECT EDITOR Gillian Roberts
ART EDITOR Deborah Myatt
MANAGING EDITOR Mary-Clare Jerram
MANAGING ART EDITOR Amanda Lunn
PRODUCTION Meryl Silbert
US EDITOR Ray Rogers

First American Edition, 1995
2 4 6 8 10 9 7 5 3 1
Published in the United States by Dorling Kindersley Publishing, Inc.,
95 Madison Avenue, New York, New York 10016

Library of Congress Cataloging-in-Publication Data

Hillier, Malcolm.
    Malcolm Hillier's color garden. – – 1st American ed.
        p.   cm.
    Includes index.
    ISBN 0–7894–0158–4
        1.   Color in gardening.   2.   Gardens– –Design.
    SB454.3.C64H55   1995
    712'.2– –dc20   95–11921
                                                                CIP

Computer page makeup by Mark Bracey and
Deborah Myatt, Dorling Kindersley, Great Britain

Text film output by The Right Type, Great Britain

Reproduced by grb EDITRICE, Italy

Printed and bound in Great Britain by Butler & Tanner Ltd, Frome and London

CONTENTS

❖

Color

❖

How color works to give different
effects has an endless fascination for
people interested in creating beautiful
surroundings. Like all abstract ideas,
color theory is easier to understand
if it is placed in a familiar context.

COLOR WHEEL

❖

Throughout all of our waking hours, we live in a world of color. Indoors and out, color constantly excites our senses. It is not really surprising, then, that color affects not just our view of life but also our moods and feelings. And yet we do not often give very much thought to color: it is so familiar that we take it for granted. We gardeners are very fortunate, I believe, to be more aware of color than most people. How easily we conjure in our mind's eye a cool glade of evergreens or the exact hue of our favorite rose. But to understand a little more about using color in interesting ways to create moods in the garden, we need a rainbow of our own and our own way of viewing it.

THE PRIMARIES

The three primary colors are red, blue, and yellow, arranged at right into a triangle. They are not made by mixing other colors: each one has its particular attributes. We're apt to see red as hot and rich; blue as cool and distant; and yellow as luminous and fresh. While red and yellow abound in the gardener's wheel, blue is not nearly as plentiful (if viewed in relative terms). This natural order of things is just as well, for red, yellow, and blue mixed in equal amounts together make a dark gray of the dullest hue.

THE SECONDARIES

The colors that are the secondaries are named green, orange, violet. These do not exist in their own right, as do the primaries, but are created by mixing pairs of the primary colors in equal amounts. Thus, green is made up from yellow and blue; orange from red and yellow; violet from red and blue. You can see the secondary colors in the picture as three individual triangles arranged around the inner primary triangle: each one spans the pair of primary colors from which it is made. Of the secondaries, green is for us the most important, for it is invariably present in the garden as foliage.

THE TERTIARIES

The primary and secondary colors are placed in the outer ring (*left*, in shadow) where the apex of each of their single triangles touches it. In the space that is left between each of them, you can make the tertiary colors by mixing each closest pair of primary and secondary colors. Thus – red and violet make purple; blue and violet create indigo; blue and green create turquoise; yellow and green make chartreuse; yellow and orange make gold; and red and orange make scarlet. These are all found in the rich world of plants except for blue-green turquoise, which is not a garden color. But, in contrast to the primary and secondary colors, they are much harder to define: no two people will imagine them as exactly the same colors.

PROPERTIES OF YELLOW

❖

Primary yellow is the most joyous color of the spectrum, shining from the warm part of the color wheel as its brightest star. Being close to white, which is pure light, yellow has great clarity; it's a forward color, one to which the eye is drawn. Seen with its neighbors lime green and gold, a warm harmony appears, encompassing apricot and egg-yolk yellow beside luminous greens.

IN A LYRICAL MOOD

A melodious mix of yellows, golds, gold-greens, and cream will bring beams of sunlight in endless succession to the garden. Soft yellow lupine spires beckon invitingly toward golden-leaved elder behind. Rose 'Golden Wings', cream Sisyrinchium, and lime green lady's mantle in the front make the picture complete.

PALER SHADES

In the upper reaches of yellow are pale lemon, primrose, and apricot. These are the mellow renderings of the gold-green, true yellow, and gold that are seen here in the band below. Lying close to white, they are colors filled with energy and light, and are the freshest of hues. All are well represented in flowers at nearly every time of year (including late winter) and give a lucid brilliance to variegated foliage year-round.

TRUE COLORS

Yellow fulfills the central role here, with golden green on its cooler left-hand side and gold to the warmer right. Gold and yellow are vital features of the garden, particularly in spring. They also bring their vibrant cheerfulness to the landscape in both summer and autumn. Golden green is found mainly in foliage, borne on trees and shrubs such as dogwood, privet, barberry, and euonymus.

DARKER SHADES

In the lower reaches of yellow are mustard yellow flanked by emerald green to the left with egg-yolk yellow to the right. These darker shades of yellow and its neighbors in the middle band absorb light. They reflect their depth of color in foliage and flowers, although mustard is least represented. Green is a constant in leaves, while egg-yolk yellow appears in a host of autumnal foliage tints.

PROPERTIES OF ORANGE

❖

O range spells excitement, dynamism, and drama, but it's a color that looks in two directions. On the downside, it subdues some colors. Purples and darker blues suffer under the influence of orange, which has the effect of dulling them, producing an overwhelming drab effect. Pure oranges are warm and gay, at their most vibrant when set against brilliant clear blues, pinks, and incisive lime greens.

FADING GLORY
The color of amber reflects the sun as it dips lower toward the autumnal equinox. During early summer, hawthorn Crataegus prunifolia is wreathed in white flowers. Clusters of bright fruit follow in hues that combine wonderfully with the burnt orange of the turning leaves. Many crabapples produce a similar effect.

PALER SHADES

Peach, apricot, and buff are the pastel variants of the true orange that sits at the heart of the square. With these shades, what may be thought of as the negative aspect of orange – its dulling effect – can be used to create beautiful muted moods. Combined with gray, old rose, or steely blue, they form vistas of soothing calm. For summer, roses, particularly hybrid teas, are plentiful in this range, and autumn has chrysanthemums.

TRUE COLORS

Pure orange, at the center of this band, has gold to the left; to the right is amber. Like all the colors related to orange, these conjure autumn at first glance, though of course there are many flowers in this range for spring and summer as well. Reinforced by the two colors at either side, orange presents a sunny and welcoming mood here – its most positive face.

DARKER SHADES

The deeper relatives of orange reveal another mood. In rust, burnt orange, and blood red the temperature climbs from comfortably warm to hot, and the pace quickens. These rich and powerful tones work best with the yellows and reds that are next to them on the color wheel. They are made somber in mixes with purple and dark blues, while white serves only to heighten their withdrawal.

PROPERTIES OF RED

❖

Primary red is a wonderful and, at the same time, difficult color to use in the garden. Because it opposes green in the color wheel, and because most gardens are full of greenery in the form of foliage, red tends to be almost too vibrant and exciting for comfort. There's little feeling of serenity around red: rather, it's a blunt jab in the ribs; no sitting at ease here, but an insistent invitation to "up and at 'em."

BOMBARDED BY COLOR

Spring isn't just a season devoted to pastel hues; few flowers have as strong a color as spring-blooming tulips. Their brilliant red and the speckled leaves that match the green-lichened bark make a truly startling combination. The velvety texture of the petals strengthens their color, so it jumps out even more.

PALER SHADES

Moving from the warm side of the color wheel into regions of cooler tones, pink is combined here with peach to its left and mauve to its right, making an oddly interesting trio. These pale hues deliver a much less demanding style of red. They mix with silver or gold foliage to conjure a mood that has an old-fashioned feel, one that is tranquil, with a slightly dusty air, yet still worthy of interest.

TRUE COLORS

Here is pure red in the center position, separating scarlet to the left side and purple to the right. This range of color can so easily jar on one's eye and grate on one's sensibilities. It's particularly the outer two that fight with each other and give rise to feelings of turmoil and chaos. Disturbing mixes mean excitement, too, so don't rule them out simply because they seem at odds with each other.

DARKER SHADES

The deep tones closely related to red are easier to respond to than those in the band above. Looking from far left to right, here are dusky dark maroon, a shade of blood red that verges on black (found in many roses and dahlias), and a wonderful deep purple-red. All of them have an inner warmth. These are colors that combine easily with red to make comfortable alliances, creating tonal mixes of rich and glowing intensity.

PROPERTIES OF VIOLET

❖

Violet takes its cue from the flower of the same name. Like the shy sweet violet, it rarely reveals a showy face unless paired with the opposing contrast of bright yellow, which gets it jumping! Violet is at the dark, moody end of the color range, as are its neighbors purple and, in particular, indigo. It's effective with blue-pink, silver, and gray, but dulls red, orange, and blue and looks muddy with them.

RETIRING ELOQUENCE
Their lilac-flushed-lavender coloring puts these pansies at the pale extremity of violet. Set among chive flowers which are just about to open, and the juicy green of stems and leaves, they make a summer planting that is stunning in its sheer simplicity.

16

PALER SHADES

Three pale associates of violet appear in this top band. Blue-pink, in the center, has lilac-blue to its left-hand side and ice pink to its right side. The marvelous soft subtle quality of these colors works best in combination with plants that have silver or gray leaves. For flowers, perennials and shrubs such as lobelia and hydrangea give all of these shades, while myriad roses grace the garden with both blue- and ice pink.

TRUE COLORS

A soft shade of pure violet lies at the heart of the square and its middle band; to its left and right are indigo and raspberry pink. While all three together form a companionable group, neither indigo nor pink make genial partners with violet on its own. A pale lemony cream introduces vitality to this mix and avoids a dispirited effect.

DARKER SHADES

The square is completed with deep violet at its core, flanked to the left by dark blue-purple and with fuchsia pink lying to its right. These regal tones of the violet range (each with a rich depth of its own) receive an extra boost when the three combine. Plants that can offer choices in these hues include geraniums, aconitums (lovely, but poisonous), delphiniums, French lavender, and roses.

PROPERTIES OF BLUE

❖

In the world of flowers, blue is a color that can excite wonder and frustration, too. Not everyone may agree but I think blue is the most beautiful of colors, perhaps because of its elusive quality. Plenty of plants described as blue betray touches of red in rogue shades of lilac and mauve. True blues worth a search include plumbago, veronicas, delphiniums, borage, and blue poppy *Meconopsis betonicifolia*.

CELESTIAL VIEW
In certain lights, with the sun high aloft and filtered through pale leaves, English bluebells can appear incredibly blue. But when the sun is lower and the light warmer, less penetratingly bright, they can assume a mauve hue. Whatever color they seem, naturalized bluebells make a sight that takes your breath away.

PALER SHADES

The pale reaches of blue show lilac to the far left, ice blue in the center. Seen near left, the subtle blue muscari represent pale turquoise, a color that is rarely found in plants. These renderings of a color that is so difficult to come by in its pure form give splendid mixes with true blue if green-tinged blues are the keynote. Plantings of lilac hues and pink-blues with blue and a touch of cream are lovely combinations as well.

TRUE COLORS

At the center, true blue reigns supreme. To the left, indigo is a shade of blue that *is* possible to get: species of *Aconitum* are an example. But the color we call turquoise, represented as silvery blue-green to the right of blue, is not a garden color. *Oxypetalum caeruleum*, a vine, is close, but at the same time manages to appear unnatural.

DARKER SHADES

Inhabiting the nether end of the blue spectrum is a somber gang. Navy blue is a center of lighter relief; deep violet to its left side, with dusty blue to its right, is darkly mysterious; all three colors are withdrawn to an extreme degree. Although they work well together, these hues are not easy to pair with many others. Red and orange, which are their opposites on the color wheel, defeat them.

PROPERTIES OF GREEN

❖

Green is the color that dominates in the garden, and if flowers colored green are rather rare (orchids are an exception), leaves abound – not only in pure green but in greens tinged silver, bronze, blue, and gold. So, it's primarily foliage that we have to thank for the abundance of garden greens. Gentle and cool, green refreshes when used alone. It's dramatic with red, and in tune with yellow and blue.

CONGRESS OF GREENS
Of all trees and shrubs, conifers display green in the widest variety. From silver- through blue-green to lime green, yellow-green and gold-green, and from palest sap green to forest green: juniper, pine, arborvitae, spruce, and cypress have them all.

PALER SHADES

The top band of green has a cool shade of turquoise blue at far left; the muscari heads represent this color, as it so rarely makes an appearance in plants and flowers. Olive green, at center, is a retiring hue. Lemon-green, lying to its right-hand side, is one of the most effective colors in the garden. It makes a very good foil for shades of blue as well as soft pastel peach, apricot, pink, and lilac.

TRUE COLORS

Rich shiny leaf green, at the heart of this square, is green showing its purest form. On its cool left side, blue-green comes close to the turquoise uncommonly seen in plants. Golden green, on the warm right side of true green, will provide sunny cheer all year in striking colored forms of evergreen shrubs and trees.

DARKER SHADES

Forest green and its closest allies finish the three places in the lowest band. Somber, matte, and light-absorbing green in center position is a color of both deciduous and evergreen foliage alike. Its solidity pleases with scarlet and orange-reds. Dark blue-green, to the left, is radiant in mixes with silver. To the right, deep golden green is vital enough to use alone.

PROPERTIES OF WHITE

❖

White is the color of light, and no more visible to us in its true, pure form than is light itself. The color that we see as white is reflected light that has other colors mixed with it in small and varying amounts. Infinite tones of white exist (white with a hint of any color you may wish to name), and the world of plants is generously blessed with them all.

Seen against other colors, white can change a great deal, so different colors of leaves as well as flowers have an effect on how we perceive white blooms. These least showy members of the garden often rely on their scent to attract the creatures that pollinate them. Rose, stock, jasmine, flowering tobacco – the list runs on. No wonder all-white plantings are so desired.

▲ TWO-TONE FEATURE
Snowball heads of viburnum stand out brilliantly against a bank of bright new green leaves. So, too, do the iris (seen in the foreground, at left), but they appear a warmer white, because of the mass of purple smoke tree leaves behind them.

◀ STARSHINE WHITE
In a boundless sea of feathery silver-blue tansy, white daisy flowers perch on their sinuous stalks and gleam like tiny stars. Vicious, spiny Agave leaves concentrate the color and add bold textural interest.

WHITE WITH GOLDEN GREEN

The white flowers at the center of each of the squares on this page are exactly the same. Each appears to be a different shade of white, depending on the color around it. Against golden green they are bright white.

WHITE WITH RICH GREEN

Surrounded by glossy rich green, white seems tinged with green. Here, the color that surrounds the white square has depth and strength, vigorous qualities that are both reflected by the white and absorbed into it.

WHITE WITH BRONZE-GREEN

Placed against bronze-green and mahogany, the white square has a much warmer feel. This effect is given by its association with red (an element of mahogany and bronze), lying on the warm side of the color wheel.

WHITE WITH WARM GRAY

A backdrop of warm gray foliage has an extraordinary, dulling effect on its center of white flowers, making them look beige and quite unattractive. Cool gray, in silver and silvery blues, would bring the white to life.

OPPOSITE CONTRASTS

❖

Colors that are precisely opposite each other on the color wheel create the strongest contrasts in the garden (and elsewhere). When opposing pairs are mixed together, however, a muddy and uninteresting shade of gray usually results.

Contrasting opposites occur between either a primary and secondary color – which means yellow and violet, red and green, or blue and orange – or a pair of tertiary colors, meaning indigo and gold, or turquoise and scarlet, or purple and chartreuse. (Page 9 explains what secondary and tertiary colors are.) In each of the pairs, the colors put against one another jump out as if they have been lit from within.

▲ QUITE CONTRARY
Orange tulips beside blue grape hyacinths make an extraordinary pairing, especially when only very little green, which would alter and diminish the effect, is visible. If a smaller quantity of one of the colors is used, the contrast is even more striking.

CONSPICUOUS ATTRACTION ▶
Against the luminous swordlike leaves of Crocosmia, the bright red dahlia flowers seem to be on fire: the green, too, is at its most vibrant. The small amount of red to greater green gives a very lively contrast.

YELLOW & VIOLET

In this pair, the same yellow is placed with violet, its direct opposite on the color wheel, and then (*far right*) with gold, a color that is next to yellow and with which it harmonizes closely. The two yellows look quite different. Against violet the yellow square is dazzlingly bright: it leaps up to meet the eye. Against the gold, though, it appears almost to withdraw and becomes more demure.

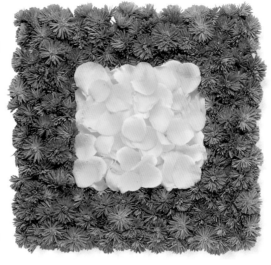 

RED & GREEN

Here is an immensely exciting pair of opposites – the heat of fiery red is set against the cool of leafy green. It seems almost impossible that this red is the same as the red that lies in the middle of harmonizing purple. On one side, the red is ablaze, but on the other seems to fade away. In the garden, the green of foliage usually offsets red, so red tends always to have even greater impact and presence.

BLUE & ORANGE

This last example of opposites made up from a primary and a secondary color is maybe the most striking of all. The tulips and grape hyacinths opposite illustrate the garden fireworks that blue and orange provide. Seen with orange, the blue is intense and vibrant, while on the square of purple (which is blue's neighbor on the color wheel) it looks quite dull and, indeed, arouses little interest.

HARMONY

❖

PURPLE

VIOLET

INDIGO

BLUE

TURQUOISE

GREEN

The color wheel offers an infinite number of combinations. Those that are pleasing and at the same time very easy on the eye are the paired colors that lie close to each other. To look at the pairs, the wheel is divided into two halves. The warmer half moves clockwise from red at the apex to lime green; the cooler half runs from green to purple. Each pair is a harmony, yet its mood changes according to its place on the color wheel. On the warmer half, red and scarlet, the hottest hues, make a vivid sound. Orange and gold are mellow but still sunny, yellow and lime green a clean-cut pair. Now beginning the cooler half are green and turquoise, the latter so rare in plants that silver-gray-blue leaves take its place. Blue and indigo are the coolest hues. Violet and purple produce a feeling of composure and restraint.

PAIRS IN THE COOLER HALF

VIOLET & PURPLE

The calm reticence of violet and purple makes these, for me, a pair with nostalgic charm. New York asters and roses capture the mood.

BLUE & INDIGO

These closest companions conjure a vision of deep water and intense summer skies. They are wonderful with the vitality of bright white.

GREEN & TURQUOISE

Foliage in all varieties of blue and turquoise creates a calm mood in the garden. Here, turquoise is seen as blue-green, silver-blue, or gray.

WARMER HALF

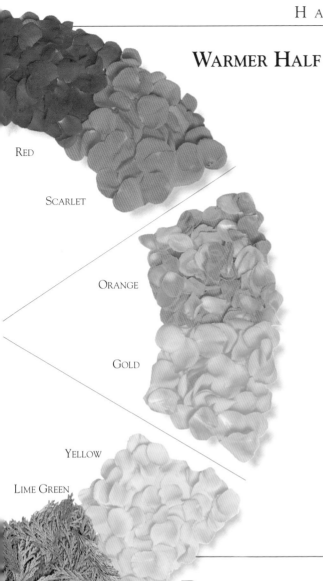

RED

SCARLET

ORANGE

GOLD

YELLOW

LIME GREEN

ON THE SAME WAVELENGTH
You can just sense the warmth of these rich dark red tulips and orange wallflowers as you look at the picture. Their appearance in spring is so welcome! Although the colors are very bright, in close harmonization they work comfortably with each other.

PAIRS IN THE WARMER HALF

YELLOW & LIME GREEN

Pure and fresh, this twosome has a sharply exhilarating edge to it. An abundance of lime green will give all the other garden colors a lift.

ORANGE & GOLD

Sweet melodies arise when orange and gold combine. They are warm and sleepy, colors of autumn that work just as well in summer heat.

RED & SCARLET

These are stunning companions, a really loud pair demanding instant attention. Not a happy mixer, red seems made for its scarlet partner.

BEAUTY IN DISCORD

There are countless mixes of color that do not rely on clear-cut contrast or harmony for their beauty. These combinations are more about juxtaposing colors in less usual – some might say, discordant – ways to produce really individual moods. A one-color garden is not everybody's taste, but one where colors unite to bring a special atmosphere is always joyous.

If working out the mixes you like most seems intimidating, buy (even beg) flowers in colors that you find comfortable to have around you, then make up your own combinations to see first hand if these colors create the mood you want. The four squares at right illustrate how this is achieved, by bringing together unusual colors in a way I think is immensely pleasing.

▲ COOL TEMPTATION
Two colors combine in this example of an offbeat pairing some gardeners might avoid, yet the mix is inspired, with pale bluish pink ornamental onions that reach up toward racemes of soft yellow Laburnum. Together they have an irresistible appeal.

▲ SUCCESSFUL MARRIAGE
Dusty pink Achillea 'Salmon Beauty' is a gentle soulmate for powder blue bellflowers. Softened into pastel shades of red and blue (that make a rather jumpy mix in their primary states), the colors play warm against cool in a delicately attractive way.

CHEERFUL MOOD

Red, pink, yellow, and lime green come together in a fascinatingly warm group that raises one's spirits. Be it spring, summer, or autumn, its exotic overtones bring excitement and a sunny aspect to a border planting.

CONFIDENT MOOD

These remind me of peaches, apricots, and nectarines glowing warm and ripe from the sun. Pale pink, gold, and fresh green: these colors radiate optimism and are wonderful, particularly when roses peak in summer.

PEACEFUL MOOD

Primrose yellow, pale pink, blue, and silver are tender colors, fresh and clear. Intense blue gives a calm and peaceful feeling to the happy mix of yellow and pink, while a little silver foliage lifts it out of the ordinary.

PENSIVE MOOD

This dusky combination of dull oranges, white flecked with raspberry pink, and metallic dusty blue inspires a picture of heat haze: drowsy late summer afternoons, a hammock swung from trees, a book cast lazily aside.

FORM AND TEXTURE

❖

Pure color does not exist on its own in the garden: it is invariably influenced by other factors. Form and texture are vital links in the way we perceive color, the mood and feeling we attribute to it. White baby's-breath gives a pointillist effect, a dainty haze. Massed, heavy white double peonies, stunning in their proud exquisite beauty, are a totally different matter.

Then there are leaves – feathery leaves or big, broad ones; layered leaves or pleated; crinkled or whorled ones. Each has an inimitable form that reflects light in a different way, and even if all the leaves were a single green, we would perceive as many greens as forms. Texture on surfaces plays a part, too. Shiny, hairy, opaque, or bloomy – all produce their unique effects.

FLEETING EFFECT ▶
Spring light illuminating this young maple spreads trails of gold across its leaves as it is caught by their serrated edges. Behind, a dark green yew withdraws into a furry pyramid, filled with shadows. Pink, blue, and lilac bluebells are scattered in dainty impressionistic patterns below the tree.

▼ FINE DISTINCTION
A wonderful effect is created by the same vivid fresh lime green, here cast into two distinct forms. Frilled and finely toothed, the almost round leaves of lady's mantle have textures that work beautifully well with the feathered young fennel plumes.

◄ BRIAR PATCH
Like the finest barbed wire, bloomy silver and rust stems of ornamental blackberry Rubus cockburnianus *entangle daffodils in a delicate cage. The rather eerie effect will be transformed when sprays of ferny leaves and lilac flowers emerge later on.*

▼ HARD EDGE WITH SOFT
These two unrelated plants are similar in makeup, with showy bracts surrounding their flowerheads. The soft forms of pink hydrangea bracts nestling around clusters of tiny flowers look perfect with the hard, spiky, metallic silver bracts of eryngium.

CRISP AND HAZY ▼
With its knobbed white-woolly stems and large silver-gray leaves, a grand specimen of Verbascum bombyciferum *creates a robust textural partnership with the vivid crispness of variegated euonymus behind.*

DISTANCE AND SCALE

❖

Color can be used for creating effects that fool one's eye. It can be especially helpful in producing impressions of distance and scale that are at odds with reality. Cool colors, dark blue-greens in particular, appear farther away than they actually are. Bright warm colors are more forward, so appear closer. (Pages 26 and 27 explain what cool and warm colors are.)

To create a feeling of length in a small garden, position yellow-flowering and foliage plants at the front, with flowers of dense blue or purple toward the back. Blue-green and darker green foliage will support the effect. Soft and muted shades of bold tones also give an impression of distance. Their misty quality is nowhere more effective than in the creation of subtle vistas.

▲ PRIMARY GAIN
Without the red poppies at its center (try covering them with a finger), this border appears extremely deep. But reveal them and they spring toward you, carrying the surrounding view along with them, and making the border seem much less deep.

◀ DISCRETE DIFFERENCE
The brownish purple haze of smoke tree Cotinus coggygria 'Foliis Purpureis' in flower retires into the background of this informal scene, while the brilliant leaves of baptisia in the middle ground bring it forward, placing it close to the onlooker.

BRAIN TEASER ▶
In this picture, the colors invite the eye into a multilayered effect that is both real and imagined. White and pink, seen in the sedum heads with the mallows and dahlias behind, pull these plants to the foreground. Dots of white and beige draw the eye to a backdrop of interesting detail.

▼ GRAND ILLUSIONS
The separate clumps of yellow here seem to be one on top of the other, creating an impression of a rather narrow border. As background meets foreground, a strange three-dimensional image emerges, where any effect of distance has been destroyed.

SEASONAL LIGHT

❖

Each of the four seasons has its own quality of light. Transitional changes are heralded by waves of plants coming new from the earth in the endless circle of life, each set reflecting the special relationship it has with the season. The clarity of spring light is echoed in flowers of yellows, blues, and pinks. Early summer has warm, hazy morning light: it buzzes excitedly.

Midsummer revels in sun at its highest, color at its sharp brightest. As summer progresses, a weary mood weighs down light and air: colors seem jaded. Autumn hums a brief color tune, washed with ethereal light at dawn, bathed in a honeyed evening glow. Winter, dressed now in blue crystalline light, then in gray, sparkles with spots of color, and life comes full circle.

WINTER LIGHT ▶

A pair of somber Irish yews impress their strong outlines on the flat silver-gray light of winter, standing like stalwart bastions against the chill. Between them, the pink bark of birch Betula ermanii *enjoys the wintry light. Such a subtle color could be lost in the glorious profusion of summer.*

▼ SPRING LIGHT

The move from winter to spring is almost imperceptible: then, a sudden awareness of young green moss – illumined by clear cool shafts of light – stirs all one's senses. In the pure thin light that is spring's own gift, these tiny nodding white snowdrop heads look like glistening drops of water.

▲ SUMMER LIGHT
The light of midsummer is flirtatious and warm, brilliant, bright, and vividly alive. With the sun now at its zenith, the light leaps and twirls. It casts strong and dark shadows as it emerges to solid blue, then sweeps across flowers in streams of gold.

◀ AUTUMN LIGHT
From the stored heat of summer, autumn releases a final joyous fling of warmth in its light. Gold, copper, rust, and burnt orange create a spectrum of color that is special to this time of year and echoed in autumn's light. Confirm the genial mood and contentment that such embered light inspires with plantings in the same hues.

DAYLIGHT TO DUSK

❖

Outside, tending to their plants, gardeners soon become familiar with the changing pattern of light through the day, and how this affects the color of flowers and leaves. In the morning, when the sun has just risen and is at its lowest, light is apt to be cool. Then, plants have superb definition, which is why morning is such a good time to photograph the garden.

At midday, the sun has climbed to its highest point, and the light is inclined to be very flat. Because shadows are lacking, the landscape is less well defined and colors can easily appear bleached out. In the evening, the sun is again low, but the light is much warmer than in the morning. Now shadows are long, so every leaf and petal stands out in renewed sharp focus.

▲ LIGHT AT MIDDAY
With the sun high, a blaze of color works well, because its rich palette is strong enough to compete with the flatness of reflected midday light. Muted tones, which can look lovely at morning or evening, lack interest when the light source is directly overhead.

▲ LIGHT AT DAYBREAK
The cool cutting edge of early morning light catches these grassy seed tassels excitingly; at midday they would appear dull. White flowers and white-marked foliage look marvelous at this time of day – worth a thought when you're creating plant combinations.

LIGHT AT EVENING ▶
In the deep, warm light of evening, a multitude of greens takes on a luscious golden glow, and beckoning shadows are cast over sun-warmed stones. I would like to enjoy this leafy scene every late afternoon, breathing in the mellow tranquility it transmits.

Spring

The first bluebells are an amazing
sight. Their clear color mirrors
the color of spring skies, spreading
peace and tranquility over grassy
slopes and wooded valleys through a
veil of dappled sunlight and shade.

PALETTE FOR SPRING

Spring is the time of regeneration, and its palette mingles the joyful colors that proclaim new life. Trees burst into a mass of translucent gold-green leaves. Grass pushes its vivid lime green blades through the bare earth. Daffodils form drifts of limpid yellow. Blossoms mix crisp linen whites with bright ice pinks. Bluebells create lakes of clearest blue. And to intensify these colors, nature adds splashes of orange, scarlet, and cerise.

Spring Sky with Japanese Cherry Blossoms
The quality of light is at its most playful in spring. It tumbles about with renewed clarity as rapid changes of weather introduce intense pale blue and scudding white to the sky. Here, a flowering cherry tree spreads a veil of snowy petals underfoot, and darting shadows illuminate both blossoms and grass.

• RED *appears in the palette for spring through a wide spectrum from luminous brights to clear pastels. Blended with the other spring colors, its soft warmth anticipates summer's richness.*

• YELLOW *is jubilation in color, breathing life into the reds, blues, whites, and greens of the season's palette. From the palest lemon to zesty vivid orange, yellow has the welcoming feel of a mood that is so well suited to this time of year.*

• BLUE, *in all its thrilling tonal variation, echoes the colors of the spring sky and of sparkling water. Set among shimmering new leaves, the calm brilliance of blue shines forth enticingly.*

• WHITE *is the color of light and purity – symbolic meanings that make it nature's own fitting choice for the season of renewal and rebirth. Whether snowy or creamy, white adds a spark that illuminates the complete palette.*

• GREEN, *in the golden glowing form of fresh young foliage, lies at the foundation of the spring palette, a continuous backdrop that gives a soft clarity to all the other colors of this season.*

FRESH GREENS

EVEN THOUGH GREEN (and particularly a vivid yellow-green) is a main part of spring's palette, in cool years and climes it can make its arrival late, as plants venture only then to unfold their leaves. Ferns, grasses, and hostas all produce prodigious quantities of lush greens. The dewy green of trees, seen at left in the graceful outlines of a Japanese maple and silver willow, is echoed in many euphorbia flowers and the snowball bush viburnum. Cherish this moment, because its brief brilliance is dulled as spring wends into summer.

TWO-TONE PARTNERS

RELATED COLOR SWATCH

This grouping mixes cooler and warmer greens in the sterile flowers and young foliage of snowball bush viburnum and hostas, and the intense golds of privet and meadowsweet leaves. Use various greens to create a relaxing focus for the eye, and a sense of tranquility that will reassure yet stimulate at the same time.

VIBURNUM OPULUS
Snowball bush viburnum. *The mophead flowers of this shrub turn almost white with age. Red autumn leaves add greatly to its garden value.* ●

RESPLENDENT SHOW OF FOLIAGE
Around a cypress tree, fern fronds unfurl as hostas, euphorbias, Ligularia, and daylilies put on a leafy display. The lime green of ostrich fern Matteuccia struthiopteris is quite astounding in its vividness, paralleled by the color of Euphorbia seguieriana.

STARTLINGLY RENEWED APPEAL
Plants that can look downcast in winter wake to lively growth. These willowy leaves of mace sedge Carex grayi, *pushing up among sweet violets, are given an extra boost by highlights of spring sun. Hakonechloa macra 'Aureola', a beautiful grass, produces fountains of striped gold-green. Its rust-colored flower spikes follow in autumn.*

LIGUSTRUM OVALIFOLIUM 'AUREUM'
Golden privet. *A dense, upright evergreen or sometimes semievergreen shrub, good for hedging and topiary.*

FILIPENDULA ULMARIA 'AUREA' Meadowsweet. *A perennial, grown for its bright young foliage that matures to pale green, and with creamy white flowers in midsummer.*

HOSTA FORTUNEI 'AUREA' Plantain lily. *A vigorous perennial, beloved of slugs as are all hostas. Trumpet-shaped purple flowers appear in midsummer.*

OPPOSITES ATTRACT

Blue with orange; yellow with violet; and red with green: when seen together, the colors that lie opposite each other in the color wheel produce the greatest contrasts. Such strong, vibrant colors excite and dazzle the eye, and their strength is heightened when they are placed in pairs, because opposites complement each other in the garden (as elsewhere). Despite the dominance of yellow in spring, many other colors are to be found – among tulips and rhododendrons in particular – that will supply a bold respite from soft spring tones.

EUPHORBIA CHARACIAS SUBSP. CHARACIAS Spurge. An upright evergreen shrub with gray-green leaves that flowers from spring into early summer.

RELATED COLOR SWATCH

The balanced effect of primary-with-secondary color pairs creates a thrilling perspective, a grand diversion into spring for tired winter gardens. Notice how these rich red Persian buttercups almost leap from the page; but try covering them with your hand and the greens appear immediately much less intense. The red would look duller, too, without the greens on either side.

STRIKE UP THE BAND
The splayed heads of lily-flowered tulip 'Golden Duchess' form a well-considered contrast to violet-blue Muscari armeniacum. Drifts of densely massed color are simple to achieve with spring bulbs, but a very formal planting tends to look uncomfortable.

RANUNCULUS ASIATICUS Persian buttercup. *A tuberous perennial that needs shelter, with single or double red, pink, yellow, orange, or white flowers in late spring to early summer.*

A QUIETER TUNE
Gentle contrasts can be just as effective as strong ones and make equally definite statements, but their subtlety has a more soothing effect. Here, orange Euphorbia griffithii 'Fireglow', flowering alongside a blue-purple Japanese iris in late spring, seems quite at ease. The informal mood is perfect for a wilder part of the garden.

BUXUS SEMPERVIRENS Common boxwood. An evergreen shrub or small tree reaching 15ft (5m). Its bright young growth makes a late spring treat.

BUXUS SEMPERVIRENS Common boxwood. *The previous years' foliage has a gloss on the uppersides that contrasts with paler matte undersides.*

A QUIET CONTRAST

Stalwart PRIMULA VULGARIS

I FIND THE COMBINATION of yellow, the high-flying color of spring, with purple, lilac, and blue-pink an immensely pleasing one. The contrast is not nearly so strident as when yellow is paired with violet, but the yellow inspires these cool shades of purple and pink and warms them with its sunny breath. Cherry blossoms, hyacinths, azaleas, camellias, rhododendrons, tulips, and primroses (*see left*) all come within this color range, and are enhanced by painterly strokes of pale and gold-green spring foliage.

RELATED COLOR SWATCH

Spring shrubs and bulbs usually flower for rather short periods. A combination that provides for a succession of overlapping colors will make the most of their soft contrasts. Golden forsythia appears at the peak of the season, blooming freely on bare stems. A variegated semievergreen privet gives year-long color, but shows its freshest face in late spring when tender new shoots emerge. The purple heads of ornamental onions and carmine-flushed single tulip 'Renown' fill in the gaps.

ALLIUM AFLATUNENSE
Ornamental onion.
A bulb flowering in late spring to early summer. The heads dry well for indoor displays.

SWEET SCENTS WITH LAVENDER
Evergreen rhododendrons have many qualities that recommend them, not least their bold foliage and fine flowers. Some gild the lily with blooms that open from distinctively colored buds. The large primrose yellow trusses of Exbury hybrid Rhododendron *'Crest', pictured here with an azalea, unfold from orange buds.*

LIGUSTRUM OVALIFOLIUM 'AUREUM' Golden privet.
A semievergreen or evergreen shrub, needing a position in full sun for its variegated gold-and-green foliage.

*FORSYTHIA x
INTERMEDIA
'SPECTABILIS'. A
deciduous shrub of
spreading habit.* ●

PINK PERFECTION
*Single-flowered cherries are, I think, the
most beautiful. It's hard to imagine any
improvement on this scene of a Yoshino
cherry* Prunus x yedoensis *spreading a
sweet-scented gauze of ice pink blossoms
over naturalized 'Fortune' daffodils.*

● *TULIPA 'RENOWN'*
Single late. *A reliable
late spring or very early
summer bulb, supplying
in each flower a muted
contrast of carmine red
and creamy yellow.*

ESSENTIAL SPRING

GOLD, YELLOW, CREAM, AND WHITE: in all their aspects of harmony, clarity, and purity, these are the colors that signal the arrival of spring. Their shining brightness spreads through the land in blossoms and blooms, while trees break into tender new foliage that is an intense lime green. Clearest blue skies, lightly broken by hurrying clouds, smile on this conspiracy of color, giving the yellows and whites even more luminous power and brilliance.

POLYGONATUM COMMUTATUM
Great Solomon's seal. *A leafy perennial bearing demure, bell-shaped white flowers in small clusters during late spring.*

TULIPA 'OSTARA'
Double late. *A peony-flowered bulb blooming in late spring.*

TULIPA 'GOLDEN APELDOORN'
Darwin hybrid. *A bulb with large single flowers from mid- to late spring.*

RELATED COLOR SWATCH

High spring sunshine bursts forth in this group that combines the rich translucent yellow tones of single 'Golden Apeldoorn' and double 'Ostara' tulips with Great Solomon's seal and the clear, pale green, young leaves of *Euphorbia polychroma*. Broom adds its joyful golden spires and breathes a honeyed scent besides.

CYTISUS x PRAECOX 'ALLGOLD'
Common broom. *A deciduous shrub with palest green leaves and masses of golden pealike flowers in late spring.*

EUPHORBIA POLYCHROMA
Spurge. *A bushy perennial with fresh yellow-green foliage. Loose heads of yellow flowers appear over a long period during the spring months.*

FLOWERY DRIFTS AMONG GRASS
Gold and white 'Fortune' and 'Kilworth' daffodils nod before a fountain of brilliant yellow Forsythia x intermedia; for a softer effect, try F. suspensa. These daffodils naturalize well in grass, if it is left unmown until after their leaves have died down.

A PLANT FOR MOIST PLACES
White skunk cabbage seems an unfortunate name for Lysichiton camtschatcensis, a beautiful perennial that likes to grow beside, or even with its feet in, water. Its large spathes emerge in spring and stand brilliantly alone before the rich green leaves unfold.

◀ SPREADING GROUNDCOVER
Fragile-looking windflower Anemone blanda *is at its most lovely in the white form nestling here before low-growing 'Jack Snipe' daffodils. Plant anemones in a spot where they can run wild: once established they soon become invasive.*

ZESTY WELCOME ▶
The stronger color tones of spring are one of its exhilarating surprises. In this classic combination of azure, emerald, gold, and deep orange, light appears to dance over the landscape, imparting a vibrancy to 'Ambergate' daffodils that is so very much a mark of early spring.

ESSENCE OF THE SEASON ▲
Demure, delicate, and refreshing, this grouping conveys a mood of pure spring, with variegated evergreen Euonymus fortunei *'Emerald and Gold' backing the silver-veined leaf rosettes and serenely reflexed flower petals of* Erythronium *'White Beauty'.*

IN A LEAFY WOODED GLEN ▲
Yellow azalea Rhododendron luteum *shines out wondrously among the lime green foliage of trees dappled with the tenuous rays of early sunshine. Its flowers, resembling those of a large honeysuckle, infuse the air with nutmeg and clove scents.*

SUBTLE WARMTH

HELLEBORUS WITH DAFFODILS

ONE OF MY favorite groupings is a range that is taken from the warm side of the color wheel. Yet even more than the colors themselves, the yellows and oranges, reds and purples, it's the tasteful variations on them – encompassing peaches and cream, apricot with ice pink, plum set against gold – that are such a delight. These produce extraordinary effects that are a little bit unusual but still easy on the eye: the spotted deep pink Lenten roses and daffodils *(left)* make a wonderful marriage. Whatever surprises spring weather brings, these color combinations spread pure joy.

RELATED COLOR SWATCH

This marvelously mellow suite is made from five late spring bulbs and shrubs. The spires of fritillary have a deep red translucent quality to their chocolate brown coloration, which is nearly matched in the bicolored broom, and faintly echoed by the pink margins of the azalea petals. Frilled and fringed salmon parrot tulips bring their bright colorful edge to the combination, while the aptly named *Spiraea japonica* 'Goldflame' binds it together with foliage of orange-red and gold.

FRITILLARIA PERSICA 'ADIYAMAN' *Fritillary. A bulb that flowers in midspring. The stems are clothed with narrow gray-green leaves.*

SPLASHED WITH SUN
Royal fern Osmunda regalis, *which can reach a stately height of 6ft (2m), unfurls its great fronds in a brilliant swath of late spring sunshine. Behind, the coral trumpets of* Rhododendron 'May Day' *spread a warm glow against their dark green leaves.*

MELODIOUS TONES

Growing in their preferred moist spot, a group of
perennial Japanese primroses exhibits a broad
variety of colors in this range. From yellows to
golds through burnt orange to mauves and faded
pinks, it's a lovely, sunny-looking, uplifting mix,
and the primroses' rosettes of pale green leaves
serve to highlight and set off the other colors.

RHODODENDRON 'CECILE'
Knap Hill azalea. *A small
deciduous shrub. The large
trumpet-shaped flowers are
● borne in late spring.*

TULIPA 'SALMON
PARROT' Parrot group.
*A bulb that produces
its typical frilly-petaled
● flowers in late spring.*

SPIRAEA JAPONICA
'GOLDFLAME'. *An upright
deciduous shrub with orange-
red young leaves becoming
● bright yellow, then green.*

● *CYTISUS SCOPARIUS*
'PALETTE' Broom. *A
deciduous shrub bearing
pealike flowers along
leafy arching branches
during late spring.*

COOL COMPANIONS

SHADES OF COLOR in cooler tones seem to be especially suited to this time of year. In this fresh, reserved combination of pale blue-pink and lilac, powder pink, mauve, white, silver, and cream, each color adds its own clear voice to produce an appropriate mood of serenity in the garden – a period of composure before rising temperatures stimulate more vibrant colors. Promote this feeling of calm continuity with plants that will step easily from spring to summer. In this range, there are many lilacs and azaleas that straddle the seasons.

WEIGELA FLORIDA. A strong-growing deciduous shrub. To maintain vigor, cut back after flowering.

RELATED COLOR SWATCH

A perfection of pinks in this collection of shrubs and perennial snakeweed (or bistort) inspires a cheerfully relaxed mood, and would make a splendid planting to cover both the end of spring and the start of summer. Weigelas often add to their bounty – and value in the garden – by producing another show later in summer.

SOFT HUES WITH STRONG ACCENTS
The neat daisy heads of Bellis perennis 'Pomponette' have an attractive woolly-ball texture that enhances their shades of soft pink and white. With them, the blue-green leaves and fringed magenta flowers of a late-flowering tulip form an easy rapport.

POLYGONUM
BISTORTA
'SUPERBUM'
Snakeweed,
bistort. A
perennial that
can become
invasive.

LIGHT-HEARTED PARTNERS
*For the smaller garden, I greatly favor
azaleas in understated pastels over those
in bold strong tones that can overwhelm.
Here, Rhododendron 'Sir Edmund' is
paired with R. 'Lavender Girl' in an
ensemble of delicately retiring beauty.*

SYRINGA 'ESTHER
STALEY' Lilac. A
*deciduous shrub. Red
buds open to scented
flowers from mid-
spring to early
summer.*

RHODODENDRON
'PURPLE TRIUMPH'
Vuyk hybrid azalea.
*An evergreen shrub
needing some shade
and shelter from cold
winds. Profuse, large
single flowers appear
during late spring.*

WHITE WITH RED

COMPANION PLANTING

W HEN RED – the most dazzling of all the colors – is viewed against white, it takes on an almost cool light: it's as if some of the heat has been drawn out of it. And white seems to become even more pure and clean in the presence of red, as the strong primary intensifies its clarity. In the garden other colors, particularly of foliage and ground and sky, divert such simple relationships. Even so the principles apply: the ox-eye daisies (*left*) look so much brighter for the lone red catchfly stalk – a natural association of plants in a wild part of the garden.

RELATED COLOR SWATCH

Nestled in between flowering stems of vanilla-scented Mexican orange blossom and dainty spiraea, deep red, dark-spotted blooms of *Rhododendron* 'Wilgen's Ruby' withdraw into a rose-pink glow that throws luminous highlights over the creamy whites and greens. In this partnership of bold contrasts, each one of the colors lends its most positive aspects to enhance the others.

CHOISYA TERNATA
Mexican orange blossom. *An evergreen shrub that flowers in late spring, often repeating in mild autumn weather.*

BRILLIANT WHITE LIGHT
Against the rich red heads of Rhododendron *'Elizabeth' and its abundant, dark sea green foliage, R. 'Beauty of Littleworth' blossoms white with a cold blue tinge. These evergreen hybrids are best planted in dappled shade close to, but not under, trees.*

56

SNOWSCAPE IN SPRING
Summer snowflake Leucojum aestivum – oddly named, for it's a spring-flowering bulb – provides a dazzling foreground to overhanging branches of Camellia japonica 'Julia Drayton', heavy with large crimson flowers that vary from rose-form to formal double. Both plants thrive in acid soil and will grow happily given a lightly shaded position.

RHODODENDRON 'WILGEN'S RUBY'. A mid- to late spring-flowering evergreen shrub.

SPIRAEA 'ARGUTA' Bridalwreath. A dense deciduous shrub wreathed in foamy clusters of tiny white flowers in late spring.

◄ DELICATE ALLIANCE
Flowering in midspring, a willow-leaved
Magnolia salicifolia *casts a mantle of*
starry white across a misty wooded back-
ground. Its fragility is further emphasized
by the almost tropical warmth and richness
of the deep crimson rhododendron blooms.

GENTLE PROVOCATION ►
White with orange-red makes for a softer
effect – one that's still exciting but a little
less intense. These tufted great umbrellas
of crown imperial Fritillaria imperialis
look really magnificent beside 'Merlin'
daffodils, whose slightly ruffled central
cups echo the color of the fritillary bells.

▼ CHANGE OF PACE
Daffodils provide many opportunities for
variations on the theme. 'Sempre Avanti'
brings dots of buff-apricot to this planting
that blur the margin of contrast between
the cardinal red of 'Ile de France' tulips
and the vivid greens of leaves and grass.

Summer

In lovely, varied textures and colors
that are vivid, soft, and subtle, a
deep border sings out the glory of the
season. At no other time of year is the
gardener presented with such an
incredible choice of bounteous gifts.

PALETTE FOR SUMMER

S ummer releases an explosion of color in the garden, and gardeners are spoiled for choice. Glorious combinations clamor against lush verdant greens. Contrasts and harmonies sing with myriad voices: demurely in white, cream, lilac, and ice pink; warmly in the sunniest of yellows, oranges, and golds; powerfully in vibrant scarlet and vermilion. And as the season wears on, the song changes to brooding tones of indigo and wine red.

EARLY PROMISE FOR A FEAST OF COLOR
Pale summer morning light illuminates the misty pinks of lilac and ornamental onion heads, leaving blue columbine in partial shade. A softly harmonizing mix emerges among the rich greens of herbaceous foliage, punctuated by darker spires of Irish yew.

- BLUES *in summer's palette often lean toward the red end of the spectrum. This leaning makes them blend especially well with the pinks and paler purples that dominate the early part of the season.*

- YELLOW *has a depth to its rich color tone that reflects the increasing warmth of the sun. All through the season, it's in harmony with orange and golden greens and forms exciting contrasts when used with violet and bluish pinks.*

- ORANGE *is at its freshest and most lively in summer. Lying sociably between red and yellow, it gives a warm and friendly effect in mixes that include these colors. In small quantities with lilac or pink or lime green, its jewel-like quality shines through.*

- PINKS *appear in varying forms from the early peony pastels to the lurid tones of high summer phlox. Then pinks fade in the glow of the first chrysanthemums. All blend happily together with the palette's other colors.*

- REDS *speak with a strong, deep velvety voice during the summer months. Luminous and startling against foliage greens, reds are dulled and forfeit much of their vitality and richness when paired with either blue or violet.*

HARMONY OF RICH PINKS

GENTEEL *DIANTHUS BARBATUS*

W ITH SUMMER COMES a host of flowers in shades set between red and purple on the color wheel. Pinks in particular go on display, and their major role in the garden lasts all season. It's easy to plan a design that encompasses these related colors, from true primary red spreading out through fuchsia pink to cherry red, cool ice pink, lilac, and mauve. Sweet William (*left*) contrives such a grouping on its own. There is a safety in harmony that inspires confidence, and you can be sure that the mood of such a planting will always be beautiful to behold in a gently undemanding way.

RELATED COLOR SWATCH

A swath of bright rich pinks will shimmer in the sun of summer. All these pinks are composed of red with the addition of either blue, black, or white. Textures play a strong part and enhance the interest in single-color plantings. The wavy velvet ruffles of *Celosia* are echoed here in the stripy pale pink petals of *Lavatera* and the layered pompon flowerheads of *Gomphrena*.

GOMPHRENA GLOBOSA Globe amaranth. *A bushy annual with pink, purple, orange, yellow, or white flowers from mid-to late summer.*

COMPLEMENTARY FORMS
The blue-pinks and pale mauves of daisylike cineraria flowers harmonize well with the dark leaves of hazel Corylus maxima 'Purpurea' in both texture and tone. Boldly outlined but subtly patterned and with a rich depth of color, the foliage is a lovely complement to the delicate forms and soft hues of the flowers.

FLEETING APPEAL
Biennial foxglove Digitalis purpurea has tall and undulating spikes of bell-shaped flowers in various pinks as well as white, all with dark-spotted throats. Cut off the stems after the short flowering period in early summer and you will be rewarded with a second showing of smaller spikes.

CELOSIA ARGENTEA VAR. CRISTATA *Cockscomb. An upright perennial grown as an annual, flowering in late summer. It includes many dwarf cultivars.* •

• LAVATERA TRIMESTRIS 'SILVER CUP' *Mallow. An erect, branching annual that flowers successively through summer into autumn.*

MASSED PLANTING ▶
Valerian Centranthus ruber *will grow
with disarming ease in the most curious
spots: the apparently inhospitable cracks
between paving slabs, or in stone walls,
are ideal domains. Here, an abundance
of its pink and brick red flowers creates
a satisfyingly integrated depth of color.*

◀ TWO IN ONE
Primula vialii *produces its own color
harmony in rich scarlet buds atop a ruff
of mauve open flowers. Grown close to
water – it likes a moist soil – the vivid
conical spikes look wondrous, poised
above clumps of their upright pale leaves.*

▼ ENERGETIC PARTNERSHIP
The intense vermilion of campion Silene
coeli-rosa *'Fire King' sits in bold accord
with purple-flowering* Verbena venosa.
Peeking up through the tangle, rain daisy
Dimorphotheca pluvialis *highlights the
strong colors with spots of white.*

◄ AGREEABLE CHOICE
Slender spires of densely clustered lupine flowers have immediate textural as well as colorful impact. Resplendent in an array of tones that runs from yellow to orange through red and pink to lilac and blue, bicolored Russell hybrids are sure to find a place in harmonizing designs.

▼ PICTURE OF HARMONY
Shades of pink that contain overtones of blue combine particularly well with lilac hues. The delicate coloration of Echium vulgare is reflected here in bluish tinged rose-pink Cosmos bipinnatus, accented by yellow centers. Rosettes of frilled and wavy-edged clarkia flowers and fine-cut, frothy cosmos foliage set off the picture.

▲ EXTENDED BOUNDARIES
In high summer, the magnificent white-striped blooms of Rosa mundi (Rosa gallica 'Versicolor') *combine with* Rosa 'Mrs. Anthony Waterer', *which flowers through the season. Their vivid crimson, combined with mauve catmint* Nepeta x faassenii, *stretches harmony to the limit.*

◀ TRANQUIL VALE
A well-contrived but still informal study in related colors. Clustered, dusty pink Phuopsis stylosa *heads that lean faintly toward blue enliven the quieter voices of lavender-hued catmint* Nepeta 'Six Hills Giant', *pinkish purple ornamental onion* Allium christophii, *and dark maroon red sweet William* Dianthus barbatus.

COTTAGE CACOPHONY

INFORMAL AND INTIMATE, the cottage garden – once a utilitarian planting of vegetables, herbs, and fruits – evolved over centuries into an exuberant, haphazard mix of edible and decorative plants. Now, to re-create the impression of cozy ease, we tend to plan our cottage gardens, combining old-fashioned favorites in colorful variety with a liberal sprinkling of herbs, but often excluding the fruits and vegetables. Unsophisticated plants will furnish the right feeling of calm disorder, set in close groups and looking casually self-seeded.

ALCHEMILLA MOLLIS
Lady's mantle. *A perennial that flowers in midsummer. Pesticide-free baby leaves are good in salads.* •

CARTHAMUS TINCTORIUS
Safflower. *A prickly leaved annual. Oil from its seeds is rich in* • *essential fatty acids.*

MONARDA DIDYMA 'BLUE STOCKING' Bee balm. *A summer perennial whose flowers and leaves are both fragrant.* •

RELATED COLOR SWATCH

This medley of golden orange with pinks and yellows conveys a distinctly cottage-garden mood. Bee balm, safflower, lady's mantle, statice, larkspur: their names ring sweet with herbal references, and the profusion of soft color shades and textural variation provides two ingredients that are an essential part of the look.

CONSOLIDA AMBIGUA 'ROSAMUND' Larkspur. A tall annual with many other cultivars in shades of blue or white as well as pink.

LIMONIUM SINUATUM 'GOLDCREST' Statice. Perennial grown as an annual. Late summer flowers, also in white, blue, pink, and purple, are excellent dried.

REASON TO BE CHEERFUL
This jovial grouping of white ox-eye daisies and spires of purple salvia, planted amid bright orange Alstroemeria Ligtu Hybrids *and yellow sundrops, lacks the strident contrast of violets and blues. It has a calm optimism to brighten the dullest of days.*

QUIET COMPOSITION
Subdued tones evoke the tranquil spirit of a cottage garden and blend with the pink-washed shutters of this charming clapboard home. Cool purple catmint Nepeta x faassenii *and sprawling mignonette* Reseda lutea *climb up by* Rosa *'Little White Pet', while mallow* Lavatera olbia *'Rosea' taps at the windowpane.*

◄ EVER-CHANGING VARIETY
At the base of a dry stone wall, a tumble of self-seeded plants (including valerian, verbascum, and daisy) produces just the haphazard mix that every cottage garden needs. It is a delightfully casual coming-together, and a wonderful combination that will look a little different each year.

▼ A LAVISH SPREAD
Much of a cottage garden's character lies in an abundance of colors and textures. Here, red and coral poppies have woven themselves in among violet bellflowers, creamy yellow Sisyrinchium striatum, and Chrysanthemum frutescens 'Pink Australian', a relatively new marguerite that has an appealing old-fashioned feel.

▲ CONTROLLED CONFUSION
Although a bit more formal, this flowery spread, in a refined palette of peach with orange and white, still has the feeling of a cottage garden. Roses can be grown over walls or arches, or as shrubs. The double blooms of rose 'Elizabeth Harkness', here surrounding shorter-lived daylilies, fill the air with their scent until autumn months.

RANDOM PLANTING ▶
The single or double cups of annual field poppy Papaver rhoeas *Shirley Series are in white to ice pink, coral and bright red. Give this delicate beauty freedom to self-seed where it chooses. Here it is scattered through miniature* Gladiolus communis subsp. byzantinus *and purple vetch.*

EVENING GLOW

W HEN THE AFTERNOON draws to an end and the sun dips low in the sky, colors take on and reflect a new light. Velvety reds and their nearest relatives begin to glow with a luminous inner warmth. Valuing this daily gift, I like to grow flowering plants near and around an outdoor sitting and eating place (where it is good to go to relax after hours of work), in an uplifting and revitalizing mix of crimson, scarlet, coral, and vivid reds. For paved or other hard areas, this color range includes many annuals that thrive in containers, which can be easily moved to create eye-catching effects.

MONARDA DIDYMA
'CAMBRIDGE SCARLET'
Bee balm. *A clump-forming perennial with deeply veined, aromatic leaves. The rich red flowers appear from mid- to late summer.*

RELATED COLOR SWATCH

Perennial bee balm combined with two different roses and annual snapdragons produces a glowing quartet of dusky companions in myriad reds. Selected with care, roses give marvelous color for a long period, although some make untidy shrubs. Introducing other plants for textural and complementary color interest besides will ensure a planting that is a delight for many months.

FLUSHED WITH WARMTH
Rose 'Living Fire' is so aptly named: in the lengthening shadows the flowers appear to burn against its gleaming dark foliage. It is most effective set toward the front of a bed, behind a mounding shrub of blue-purple, such as Lavandula 'Grappenhall' here.

PLAY OF LIGHT AND SHADOW
The salmon and red-pink blooms of climbing rose
'Aloha' furnish a custom mix of color in low as
well as brighter light. Sweet alyssum Lobularia
maritima – spreading white below – echoes their
delicious fragrance, and flowers all summer long.

ANTIRRHINUM MAJUS PRINCESS SERIES
Snapdragon. *A perennial grown as an*
annual, with bicolored flowers from
early summer until autumn.

ROSA 'NATIONAL TRUST'
Hybrid tea. *A bush rose*
producing masses of lightly
scented double flowers from
summer to autumn.

ROSA 'NORWICH CASTLE'
Floribunda. *A free-flowering*
rose that fades from deep
coppery orange to apricot.

◄ AT THE CLOSE OF DAY
Pushing upright from a sea of cut-leaved foliage, the brilliant gaudy scarlet blooms of Papaver orientalis 'Allegro Viva' are caught, gleaming, in late afternoon sun. Lobelia cardinalis would make a show of equal fire and throws splendid sword-shaped, purple leaves into the bargain.

RADIANT WARMTH ►
There is no missing the penetrating pink of phlox 'Sir John Salmon' and its near-fluorescent quality as dazzling sunbeams flood over. Verbascum rises against giant thistles behind the phlox, with evergreen Jerusalem sage mounding in front.

▲ GENTLE PURPLE BATHED WITH LIGHT
The blazing red heads of Lychnis chalcedonica are satisfyingly juxtaposed with slender stems of purple sage Salvia x sylvestris, which might otherwise appear a rather somber color. Deep red rose 'The Herbalist' would also suit the mood of quiet restraint.

▲ GLOWING HUES JOSTLING FOR ATTENTION
This border sings out cheerily against the shadows of smoke tree Cotinus coggygria 'Purpureus': the lack of light presents no obstacle. Flowering tobacco, verbenas, snapdragons, penstemons, dahlias, and amaranth vie with each other to dominate the scene.

TRANQUIL VISTAS

ALLIUM, AQUILEGIA, NEPETA

COMBINING SOFT COLOR TONES and delicate textures in flowers and foliage is an effective way to create a design that takes in any kind of view. It may be a path, a vista through to fields or across a valley, or just to a wild planting: the idea is to get from the view the lazy feeling that spells sleepy late afternoons at the peak of summer. Pictured left, feathery spheres of ornamental onion lift their heads among nodding columbines, fade into a filigree of airy catmint spires, and draw the eye back to settle quietly on hedging of dark green. All come together in a three-layered harmony of somnolent restfulness.

RELATED COLOR SWATCH

Branching spires and plumes in gentle shades suggest, by their natural forms, a mood of languorous content. Here, milkweed, love-in-a-mist with its delicately cut foliage, loose flowerheads of aromatic dill, floribunda rose 'Ainsley Dickson', and delphinium 'Loch Leven' conjure the atmosphere in mellow golds, misty pinks, smoky blues, veiled creams, and muted foliage greens.

ASCLEPIAS INCARNATA
Milkweed. A hardy tuberous perennial. The stems exude a milky sap, giving rise to the common name.

NIGELLA DAMASCENA
'MISS JEKYLL' Love-in-a-mist. A summer annual that grows fast. Decorative seed pods follow the flowers.

INVITATION TO A PEACEFUL PLACE
The misty pink blooms of Tamarix help this deep border fade away to distant hedges and trees. Smoke tree, tall thistles, and rose 'The Fairy' join with Jerusalem sage Phlomis fruticosa, artemisia, and phlox to bring about the desired effect.

HILLS AND VALLEYS
Deep sultry colors leading to paler ones present a layered view through to fields. To help create an impression of looking through divided hills, choose shrubby roses that will grow to the desired height, with some forming small low mounds and others to rise taller at the sides. Planted in between the roses, low artemisias and lavenders obscure their stems and fill the air with the drowsy hum of bees.

DELPHINIUM 'LOCH LEVEN'. *A perennial with generously endowed flower spikes to 3ft (1m) tall.*

ANETHUM GRAVEOLENS Dill. *An annual herb that has edible flowers, leaves, and seeds.*

ROSA 'AINSLEY DICKSON' Floribunda. *A vigorous summer-to-autumn selection.*

▲ HOSPITABLE HAVEN
Carefully organized disarray invests this
sunny garden room with a feeling of filmy
space, and the aromatic foliage spreading
beneath purple wallflower and columbine
is a joy to walk through. Bold, acid green
Euphorbia characias *engage the eye and*
draw it subtly back toward a dark hedge.

GENTLE SASHAY ▶
Resembling clusters of fruit drops in dusty
hues, plumed lupine spikes emerge from a
tangle of foliage and rough grass to sway
elegantly into the distance. These Russell
hybrid lupines produce their best colors if
they are grown in light, not too rich soil.

◀ SEASCAPE WITH PLANTS
Pelargoniums of all sorts, long-flowering
blue marguerite Felicia amelloides, *and*
graceful Madonna lilies with poppies and
gazanias beckon the eye down steps to the
seashore: a pointillist planting of annuals
in an idyllic setting of unrivaled allure.

BLUE SUMMER MAGIC

PENETRATING BLUE POPPY

I THINK THAT BLUE is the most special color in the garden. There are not many flowers with good blue coloring (which perhaps explains their favored place), although there are very many often described as blue that are in fact purple- or lavender-blue. *Meconopsis betonicifolia*, shown left, is a true blue of outstanding quality. Coming from the cool side of the color wheel and traditionally associated with spiritual things, blue conjures a mood of innermost peace. It's a delight with pink, cream, lemon yellow, and silver, but dull and flat in red and purple partnerships.

RELATED COLOR SWATCH

This quartet of plants has an inspired touch and is no less magical for its lack of a true blue. At far right, sea holly *Eryngium alpinum* has metallic silver-blue bracts reflected in the white eyes of delphinium 'Blue Nile'. Between and to the left, agapanthus and cornflower (caught in shafts of light) add shades of mauver blue.

CENTAUREA CYANUS
Cornflower. A branching, fast-growing annual that flowers through summer and into early autumn in reds, pinks, purples, and white as well as blue.

MAGNIFICENT MASS PLANTING
Grown in neutral and alkaline soils, the flattened open heads of lacecap Hydrangea macrophylla 'Blue Wave' will bloom lilac or pink. Only acid soil encourages such an incredible exhibition of pure blue, which will last for a long period from midsummer.

STATELY REGALIA ON DISPLAY
Delphiniums reign supreme in all their rich variety of blue. Lit from behind, delphinium 'Fenella' has a superb depth of color, overwashed with purple and intensified by each flower's black center.

DELPHINIUM ELATUM 'BLUE NILE'. *A perennial that bears its semidouble flowers on spikes to 27in (69cm) tall.* •

AGAPANTHUS CAMPANULATUS. *A clump-forming perennial producing strong erect stems of profuse rounded flower clusters.* •

ERYNGIUM ALPINUM *Sea holly. A perennial with deeply toothed foliage and, in summer, conical flowers surrounded by dramatic* • *feathered silver-blue bracts.*

83

◀ PEACE OFFERING

A gift of nature: in cracks in stone steps,
china blue speedwell Veronica prostrata
and pale lavender bellflower Campanula
garganica *have seeded themselves into a*
colorscape of rare magic. In a fine foam
of lime green, lady's mantle Alchemilla
mollis *enlivens the otherwise cool effect.*

BRIGHTER VISION ▶

The luxuriant cream-striped leaves of Iris
laevigata *'Variegata' make a background*
for its flowers that throws their soft lilac-
blue into sharp relief and shows them off
to perfection. This beardless Japanese iris
sometimes flowers again in early autumn.

▲ BOON COMPANIONS

Apricot pink rose 'Paul Shirville' casts its sensuous soft warmth
over the cool blue of love-in-a-mist Nigella damascena. *Sweet-*
scented daylily Hemerocallis *'Prairie Sunset', with* Consolida
ambigua *'Blue Spire', could make just as agreeable partners.*

▲ GRAPHIC GROUP

Sculpted out of steely blue, sea holly Eryngium x oliverianum
is a striking sight in late summer with its egg-shaped flowerheads
and delicately spiked silver bracts. Its deep-cut leaves and those
of variegated New Zealand flax emphasize the dramatic effect.

MUTED HUES

*PHLOX PANICULATA
'SKYLIGHT'. An upright
perennial flowering in late
summer. It is best grown
in a rich, moist but well-
drained soil.* •

WHEN SUMMER BESTOWS the pleasure of its balmiest days, the fresh and hazy early morning air seems to shimmer with a watchful charge. It's a time of great beauty, when even bold colors look muted. The mood is one of expectation and drowsy optimism. I like to bring about this feeling, so that it need not rely on weather or time of day, by using a misty palette restricted to pinks, lilacs, mauves, purples, and silvery grays. Delicate plant textures complement the subtle color range and help support the illusion.

RELATED COLOR SWATCH

This group will send a cool breeze wafting over the most sultry summer landscape. Layers of frilled petals and feathery spires are the perfect textural adjunct to the understated lavenders, deep mauves, warm pinks, and silver-green seen in phlox, *Lavandula angustifolia* 'Hidcote', *Dianthus* 'Doris', and evergreen *Santolina*.

SALUTATION TO THE DAY
Placed against heads of purple coneflower Echinacea purpurea *'Robert Bloom',* Perovskia atriplicifolia *sends its silver foliage and blue-gray flower spires curling toward the sky, like ribbons of smoky mist that rise at dawn.* Perovskia *is a subshrub that will bloom to midautumn, outlasting the summer coneflowers.*

MODESTLY SUPPORTING STRUCTURES
A planting of mauve Geranium 'Johnson's Blue' lies agreeably quiescent behind close-knit clumps of pink Dianthus 'Little Jock' with their dainty, spice-perfumed flowers. Spiky silver-green dianthus leaves and the hard gray stone of the path anchor both plants in their stronger textures.

LAVANDULA ANGUSTIFOLIA
'HIDCOTE' Lavender. *An evergreen shrub that forms a dense mound and is covered with flowers from mid- to late summer.*

DIANTHUS 'DORIS'
Modern pink. *A compact perennial. The abundant flowers are deeply scented and excellent for cutting.*

SANTOLINA CHAMAECYPARISSUS
Lavender cotton. *An evergreen shrub with bright yellow, button-like flowerheads in mid- and late summer, and aromatic foliage.*

◄ A FANCIFUL VISION
Elemental colors mix in a hushed reverie of dusty rose meadowsweet Filipendula rubra, *steely blue bellflower* Campanula lactiflora, *and the large bronze leaves of plantain* Plantago major *'Rubrifolia'*.

GOSSAMER LIGHT ►
An ornamental onion bears its pompons of violet-gray aloft through a fine mist of artichoke Cynara scolymus. *Edging to meet them, the fluffy floss pink spikes of steeplebush* Spiraea tomentosa *will keep their dried flowers right until winter.*

▼ CURIOUS COMPANIONS
In an unexpected yet comfortable alliance of forms, elegant fluted mallow Lavatera trimestris *'Pink Beauty' grows beside the elongated flowerheads and greenish white bracts of sea holly* Eryngium giganteum.

SERENE IN WHITE

WHITE IS THE COLOR of true light, and has always been regarded as the symbol of purity and innocence. It is also refined and elegant. No wonder that we should choose to plant entire gardens with all-white flowers. Against the glorious diversity of foliage greens, white stands out distinctively. On hot summer days, white flowers chasten the sun's glare with their cool freshness; in shade, they speak with inspiring eloquence. Even a small part of a garden planted in white will lend its composed beauty to the whole. As an added pleasure, there are many white flowers that count sweet perfume among their other charms.

MYRTUS LUMA Myrtle. An evergreen shrub that is in flower from mid- to late summer.

RELATED COLOR SWATCH

White flowers look particularly good among differing greens. Dark green makes them look spotlessly white, while gold foliage gives them a touch of warmth. Use a mix of texture, associating dots of tiny flowers with larger-petaled ones, spheres with spires. Here *Myrtus luma*, an aromatic myrtle, is placed alongside *Lavatera*, with *Ammi visnaga* and an intensely scented phlox.

SHORT BUT SWEET
Philadelphus 'Belle Etoile', sadly beloved of aphids, more than makes up for this shortcoming with a profusion of most fragrant flowers opening among still-fresh young foliage in early summer. A curtain of gold- and blue-greens behind intensifies its beauty.

90

BASKING IN REFLECTED GLORY
Love-in-a-mist Nigella damascena *'Persian Jewels' blooms blue or pink, besides the dazzling white that is here so effectively paired with silver artemisia. Sweet rocket* Hesperis matronalis *and* Geranium clarkei *'Kasmir White' would also sit well in a planting of this planned cottagey type.*

LAVATERA TRIMESTRIS
'MONT BLANC'
Mallow. A branching annual with abundant flowers from summer
● *to early autumn.*

AMMI VISNAGA. *A self-seeding annual. It bears its blooms in mid- to late summer among feathery aromatic foliage. An*
● *excellent cut flower.*

● PHLOX PANICULATA
'FUJIYAMA'. *A perennial, also listed as 'Mount Fuji', with fragrant flowers in late summer.*

IMMACULATE WHITE ▶
Rosa 'Wedding Day', nearly clouding an iron cupola, furnishes a bountiful display in early summer with Lychnis coronaria 'Alba', tradescantias, and cistus. Stately delphiniums, just visible, appear behind.

◀ FLOWERY TRELLIS
In stalky fountains, Crambe cordifolia (a delicate garden sea kale) bursts above a mound of hostas and its own leaves. It makes a gracious partner for white roses: the bourbon 'Boule de Neige' and rugosa 'Schneezwerg' are two of my favorites.

▼ COOL COMPOSURE
A contained planting of Osteospermum 'Whirligig', golden-leaved Helichrysum petiolare, and Lilium longiflorum with Nicotiana alata 'Lime Green'. Tendrils of everlasting pea wave airily over them.

VIVACIOUS YELLOWS

CLEAR AND FRESH, yellow spells out a stirring affirmation of life's excitement whenever it appears. At this time of year we see yellow and its close neighbors – gold, pale orange, and lime green – playing a spirited, even audacious part, reflecting the sun's brilliance on bright days, triumphing gloriously over dull ones. Place yellow flowers and golden foliage together for a dual feel-good effect that will lift the most somber of moods.

LIGUSTRUM OVALIFOLIUM 'AUREUM' Variegated privet. A semievergreen shrub that needs a site in full sun to keep its variegation.

RELATED COLOR SWATCH

This joyful association in gold and yellow is just right for a sunny position. Many yellow plants have an easy simplicity that cheers but doesn't invite frenzy. Here, variegated *Ligustrum* leaves incline toward floribunda roses, which are set between gold *Achillea* heads and soft-plumed *Centaurea* with loosestrife spires beside.

GILT-EDGED SPLENDOR
Towering stems of mullein Verbascum bombyciferum *grow up rapidly from their rosetted silver-gray evergreen leaves, and look particularly spectacular against an emerald green hedge. Daylily* Hemerocallis *'Golden Orchid' in front adds a mellow warmth.*

ISLAND IN A SEA OF GOLD
In a feathery bank, white Crambe cordifolia *and
silver artichoke foliage rise tall behind a golden
lemon sea of yarrow* Achillea 'Coronation Gold'
and whorled Jerusalem sage Phlomis fruticosa.

ROSA 'HARVEST FAYRE'
Floribunda. *A shrub rose
flowering from midsummer
until late autumn.* •

CENTAUREA
MACROCEPHALA
Knapweed. *A clump-
forming perennial.* •

ACHILLEA
FILIPENDULINA 'GOLD
PLATE' Yarrow. *A tall
perennial growing to 4ft
• (1.2m) or more.*

LYSIMACHIA VULGARIS
Yellow loosestrife. *An
often invasive perennial
with long-lasting flower
• spires through summer.*

VARIATIONS ON YELLOW

YELLOW IS AN EASY MIXER, shining happily alongside most other colors. With violet, its contrasting partner on the color wheel, yellow is at its most vibrant; with close neighbors red and orange it makes the most melodious mix; so too with green. Elegant beside the tranquility of blue, yellow gets from white its pure ethereal innocence. And although I have frequently heard said that yellow and pink have no place together in the garden, I look upon the two of them as well-matched, genial bedfellows.

ASCLEPIAS TUBEROSA
Butterfly weed. A vigorous perennial that grows from a taproot. Large pods follow the flowers. •

HELIANTHUS ANNUUS 'TAIYO' *Sunflower. An erect, leafy annual. It grows rapidly and will* • *reach 4ft (1.2m).*

RELATED COLOR SWATCH

A favorite composition of mine, bright orange, deep gold, and cream with glowing pink is a color mix to be treasured. The first three are culled from the warm side of the color wheel and make beautiful harmony. Reflecting their soft hues with its overtones of palest peach, pink (also a warm color) adds interest to the group without the introduction of discordant notes.

CHELONE OBLIQUA *Turtle-head. A perennial needing part shade and moist soil, flowering in mid- or late summer until autumn.*

ROSA 'MCGREDY'S YELLOW' *Hybrid tea. A small shrub that bears fragrant double flowers continuously over a long period. Good for planting in groups.*

HEIGHT OF COLORFUL EXCITEMENT
White foxgloves, highlighted by dark green, form a soft backdrop to this gorgeous planting. Brilliant yellow daylily Hemerocallis lilio-asphodelus *is splendid with bright green ligularia, intense orange Primula 'Inverewe', and ice blue* Myosotis caespitosa.

EMPHATIC DISCORD USED TO GOOD EFFECT
The sumptuous, rich shades of bluish red gladiolus and deep lilac Erysimum sit companionably together, while warm yellow heads of mullein interrupt their harmony with a wanton gleam. Here, the combination of plants has been cleverly chosen in somewhat jarring tones, so that a small proportion of yellow will spark and bring an even greater degree of verve to the surrounding colors.

◄ RESONANT BALANCE
*An offbeat plantscape of cool with warm,
in which the violet-blues of* Agapanthus
and bellflower Campanula *chorus in a
minor key, stirring up vibrations against
the oranges and yellows. The view would
have less life without so clear a contrast.*

SNUG OUTLOOK ►
*Golden Spanish broom meets bluish pink
sidalcea in a confidently energetic color
mix. A backing of solid rich dark green is
an ideal foil. Silver foliage and pale peach
poppies that seem to float add light relief.*

GLITTERING NEIGHBORS ▼
*Strong, bright yellow coreposis grows in a
luminous pool by straggling drifts of vivid
carmine campion flowers set atop slender
silver stems. Even on dreary days and in
shade, the colors will be jewel-like bright.*

A PURPLE CONTRAST

ENGAGING COMPETITORS

Purple is the richest and most opulent of hues. Since early times it has been the symbol of status, a color of preference denoting rank and nobility. Opposite purple in the color wheel, the range of yellows (brilliant stars of the spectrum) have a luminous strength of their own. When the two come together, fireworks fly. Such intense contrasts are stimulating at first, but best used in relatively small quantities. A great swath of *Euphorbia polychroma* and deep magenta cranesbill *Geranium psilostemon* (*see left*) could be too much of a good thing in a small garden.

RELATED COLOR SWATCH

Warm and cooler purples mingle with deep and clear yellows in a startling mix for a midsummer border. Gladiolus 'Golden Standard', at right, is coolly defiant against the light-absorbing quality of purple larkspur. Alstroemeria and statice, near left, are less violent in their reaction, and enjoy a more cordial relationship.

MUTUAL SATISFACTION
Subdued purple heads of ornamental onion Allium christophii and radiant Chrysanthemum segetum 'Golden Gem' with its emerald foliage meet in a symbiosis of color. The gold enlivens the purple that in turn endows the gold with greater brilliance.

LIMONIUM SINUATUM Statice. A perennial grown as an annual, flowering in summer and early autumn. It has an untidy habit. ●

FAIR CONTEST
Monkey flower Mimulus luteus *has snapdragon-like flowers of rich yellow matched for strength in the intense purple of catmint* Nepeta x faassenii. *In plantings of such bold color contrast, textural variety helps to prevent an overwhelming effect.*

CONSOLIDA AMBIGUA IMPERIAL SERIES Giant larkspur. *A hardy annual. The long flower spikes can* ● *reach 4ft (1.2m).*

GLADIOLUS 'GOLDEN STANDARD'. *A hybrid growing from a corm, with flowers from* ● *midsummer to early autumn.*

ALSTROEMERIA LIGTU HYBRIDS Peruvian lily. *A tuberous hardy perennial* ● *that dislikes disturbance.*

REGAL MAJESTY

THE COLORS OF POMP and splendor are wonderfully represented in the plant world. The rich velvety reds and purples of roses, gladioli, and clematis along with the scarlet of poppies and dahlias combine to conjure a feeling of glorious majesty that reigns over the garden in summer. Plants with purple foliage, such as *Cotinus coggygria* 'Royal Purple', *Weigela florida* 'Foliis Purpureis', and *Lobelia* 'Cherry Ripe', will emphasize the effect and create a planting of true magnificence.

CELOSIA ARGENTEA 'PLUMOSA' Feather *or* Plume cockscomb. *An annual with flowers in late summer, good for a border or containers.*

RELATED COLOR SWATCH

This stately group of plants, ceremoniously arrayed in sumptuous shades of crimson, cerise, and purple-pink, flowers at the same time near summer's end, bringing rich late-season color to rejuvenate the garden. The roses begin earlier and must be regularly deadheaded and given one feeding of rose fertilizer once their first flush is finished to ensure successive shows of flowers.

THE IRREPRESSIBLE ALLURE OF RED
Scarlet Oriental poppy Papaver orientalis *has surely one of the most potent reds of any flower. The delicate frilled petals, each with a dark maroon blotch at the base, are exhibited high above a rosette of green leaves and give way to silver-gray seed heads. Blue borage* Borago officinalis *is seen, just opening, in front.*

ROYAL FLUSH
Few sights could be more opulent than this superb pairing of dark purple clematis 'Maureen' twined among heavy stems of deep cerise climbing rose 'Pink Perpétué'. Both offer a rich display in early to midsummer, and then again late in the season.

LIATRIS SPICATA
Gayfeather. A perennial *that produces its densely clothed long flower spikes in late summer.*

GLADIOLUS 'JO WAGENAAR'
Large-flowered hybrid. *Has mid- to late summer flowers with a velvet sheen.*

ROSA 'ROUNDELAY' Modern shrub. *Bears intensely perfumed flowers, which open flat, from early summer to autumn.*

◄ COURTLY GROUP
Large and glossy blue-green leaves add a special luster to the vivid crimson many-petaled flowers of 'L.D. Braithwaite', a new English rose. Cranesbill Geranium psilostemon, *with its black-eyed, bright magenta flowers, and crimson campion* Lychnis coronaria *complete the picture.*

▼ VULNERABLE GLORY
In a similarly royal vein, the strong red Dahlia 'Alvas Doris' has generous orbs composed of many slender pointy petals; purple Verbena patagonica provides a sea of color and texture that is a perfect foil. Both have a short splendor in much of North America because neither will tolerate temperatures below freezing.

▲ DIGNIFIED ESTATE

A magical garden combines its coroneted arbor with plants that seem as if chosen for their regal colors. Among foliage of lush green, lupines stand majestically tall. Palest pink old-fashioned roses, opening from deeper buds, take center stage with violet delphiniums and frame a stunning vista through to an amphitheater of trees.

ROSY OUTLOOK ▶

Royal 'Queen of Denmark', an old alba rose that's not difficult to grow, bears an abundance of its stately pink blooms in a single longish season during the height of summer. It forms a fine background here for Lychnis coronaria, *which has silver stems wreathed in rose-crimson flowers.*

EXUBERANT SUMMER

A VOLUPTUOUS MIX of strong and vibrant colors is a thrilling sight in the garden. Glowing reds, yellows, and oranges encapsulate summer in their rich bold tones. Planted in generous groups to create a landscape of undulating hills and valleys, they brim with a mood of summer plenty, and sit easily beside the cooler purples, blues, and pinks that relieve too strident an effect. This is the sort of planting that will excite your senses, and in sunny heat radiates with the sheer joy of color.

LYSIMACHIA VULGARIS
Yellow loosestrife. A *long-flowering, clump-forming perennial that can be invasive.*

RELATED COLOR SWATCH

When colors of great intensity abound, greens play a major part. They make reds, oranges, and bright pinks leap forward, and take cool colors, in particular blue, into the background. Shades of gold- and lime green, as in bells of Ireland *Molucella laevis*, at far right, bring most colors vitality. Silver-gray and bronze send colors into hazy retreat, and work much better with soft hues.

HEART-WARMING REFRAIN
Mounding orange pot marigolds, lit up by feverfew Tanacetum parthenium *'Aureum' with its white daisy flowers and radiant emerald green foliage, join a rousing chorus in this long border with purple and yellow pansies, red fuchsias, and copper roses.*

JOYFUL ABSTRACT
Marvelous painterly effects are achieved with various mound-forming plants placed in blocks of brilliant solid color. In front, at left, rose-pink and crimson zonal geraniums merge into purple-blue Convolvulus mauritanicus. Scarlet poppies and vermilion valerian resound against broad drifts of perennial wallflower Erysimum 'Orange Flame'.

ROSA 'EDEN ROSE'
Hybrid tea. *A deciduous shrub with a profusion of scented flowers from early* ● *summer to autumn.*

AGERATUM HOUSTONIANUM
'PINKIE' Floss flower.
● *Midsummer annual.*

● MOLUCELLA LAEVIS
Bells of Ireland. *An annual. Its lime green calyces surround tiny scented white flowers.*

CALENDULA OFFICINALIS
Pot marigold. *A freely self-seeding annual with* ● *a pungent, tangy aroma.*

LUSH PARADISE ▶
Acting as foils to the purplish pink daisy flowers of Senecio pulcher, Euonymus japonicus *'Ovatus Aureus', burnt rose* Leucothöe *'Flamingo', and* Phormium tenax *'Variegatum'* (New Zealand flax) *combine in a mix of subtropical flavor.*

◀ DARING DISPLAY
A planting of strawflower Helichrysum bracteatum *has a graphic simplicity. It's the inclusion of pink among the sunshine yellows, oranges, and reds that lifts it to the height of extraordinary flamboyance.*

▼ WHITE HEAT
Terraced chrysanthemums in white, ice pink, and primrose yellow present a cool contrast to extravagant gold and orange red-hot pokers Kniphofia, *intermingled with the rich cerise of* Watsonia *in front.*

BRIGHT RED DAZZLERS

BOLD AND SASSY, red is the most forward of colors. Placed with green, the color that lies directly opposite it in the color wheel, it's even more so: it seems to leap out at you, almost with a life of its own. I enjoy red most of all used this way. Even if the combination is small scale, for instance plants in a container or a red climber festooned among the luxuriant green foliage of a tree, the effect always elicits an excited response. The strongest impact comes when shades of brilliant red veering somewhat toward orange rather than pink are set against dark glossy greens that resonate with their intensity.

IMPATIENS WALLERIANA BLITZ SERIES Impatiens. An annual that flowers from early summer to first frost.

RELATED COLOR SWATCH

This unsophisticated grouping combines just a pair of plants. They are a perfect choice for a container in a semishaded or even shaded position, and would bring vibrancy to a lackluster corner. Both the fast-growing impatiens (*far left*) and the tuberous begonia provide a lively color contrast from early summer right through to autumn. Scented flowering tobacco *Nicotiana alata* and fuchsias would also suit such a contained planting.

TUBEROUS BEGONIA 'CLIPS'.
Excellent for containers, this
B. x tuberhybrida (Multiflora
group) bears large double flowers
on sturdy stems.

DAZZLING CONTRAST
Brilliant scarlet nasturtium Tropaeolum speciosum *clambers up into a dark green yew hedge. It's a real dazzler that needs to be planted about 10in (28cm) deep in rich acid soil with roots in shade and flowers in sun. Once established, it's unstoppable.*

SHOWY CREVICE PLANTING
Give red valerian Centranthus ruber *a rocky crevice in which to grow (particularly near the sea) and it will romp away with abandon. Not so intense a red as some, its massed flower spires still create a fiery show against a strong background of greenery.*

CONSTANT GREEN

GARDEN SALAD GREENS

ELEGANT, COOL, AND SERENE, green is a constant factor in the garden, particularly in summer months, imparting a sense of well-being. It can be there as a lush leafy background to show off the myriad colors of flowers, and it can be there in its own right. A host of plants are used and valued for their leaves alone. Even plants as common as lettuce and cabbage (*left*) can play a decorative role. Use foliage in all its forms to experiment with each separate effect it creates: golden green gives life to colors; rich green intensifies them; copper and purple make red, blue, and yellow dull, even lackluster.

RELATED COLOR SWATCH

Greens come together in an intriguing mix to create a gentle muted mood. Bronze, silver, subtle plum-tinged gray, and white-with-green tempt the eye with visions of healing repose. Mingled with evergreens in a sunny mixed foliage border where flowers take only a minor part, such greens will look beautiful through the year.

UNDER SPREADING LEAFY TREES
Bright leaves of golden locust Robinia pseudoacacia *'Frisia'
stand out against the rich green backdrop of trees and the band
of dark yew hedge below. They hold their springlike color until
late autumn, and are one of the last trees to lose their leaves.*

AROUND A MOSSY PEBBLE-EDGED POOL
A shady woodland edge is a wonderful place for a grouping of special foliage plants. Bright lemon-splashed variegated hostas, lime green ostrich fern Matteuccia struthiopteris, *and cut-leaved sinuous Japanese fatsia* Fatsia japonica *recede into the cool glaucous blue of* Hosta sieboldiana.

COTINUS COGGYGRIA 'NOTCUTT'S VARIETY' *Smoke tree. Mature dull green foliage is set off by tender young leaves that open red-bronze.*

SENECIO 'SUNSHINE'. *A mounding evergreen shrub bearing small yellow flowers in summer. The youngest leaves are the most silver.*

SALVIA OFFICINALIS 'PURPURASCENS' *Purple sage. The textured purple-tinged new leaves are held on violet stems.*

EUPHORBIA MARGINATA *Snow-in-summer. An annual with showy white bracts surrounding tiny flowers.*

◀ ENCHANTED KINGDOM
A composition in greens is ideally sited at the edge of a feathery canopy of conifers on a hillside. Astonishing blue-green and bright green join in a quiet, calm world of hostas, ferns, grasses, and rhododendron.

DAPPLED SUNSHINE ▶
Variegated Russian comfrey Symphytum x uplandicum 'Variegatum' has cream-margined leaves throughout summer that seem almost like dappled sunshine against their backdrop of golden American elder.

▼ COOL PROSPECT
Sunbeams dance and cast their spell over a shady glade of ferns, irises, grasses, and candelabra primroses. Coppery green flax Phormium tenax 'Purpureum' gives the planting an upswing of dramatic interest.

PEACEFUL PASTELS

LAVATERA 'BARNSLEY'

MY FIRST SIGHT of an early summer alpine meadow was in northern Italy. Its beauty was breathtaking, an impressionistic dream made up of mostly pastel colors. Bringing this vision into the garden is very simple, for these colors, which are full of light, take to each other like rosy-flushed peaches mixed with thick, rich cream. Lemon and apricot; confections in soft rose (the mallow at left) and other quiet pinks; pale lilac, silver-blue, and of course not forgetting white: all or any of them mingle with ease in a picture of great loveliness and unerring quality.

RELATED COLOR SWATCH

A soothing group in which the lilies' stamens provide the strongest color, a bold, zesty orange reverberating against sumptuous hollyhock in an apricot shade that looks rich beside the ice pink lily petals. Here too are lilac statice (easy to grow and ideal for drying), white gooseneck loosestrife spikes, and greenish gold dill.

LYSIMACHIA CLETHROIDES
Gooseneck loosestrife. A
perennial that spreads freely. ●

A CHEERFUL PATHWAY
Pinks, yellows, and white spill out over a path: their soft colors sit well with the texture of brick. Daisy Erigeron mucronatum, at left, blooms for months, and the abundant honey gold flowers of meadow foam Limnanthes douglassii are rarely far behind.

● *LIMONIUM SINUATUM*
Statice. *An open-growing
perennial treated as an
annual. Seed is available
for many single colors.*

WATERSIDE CONTEMPLATION
*Beside a dark pond, Hosta sieboldiana proudly
flourishes its magnificently corrugated silver-blue
leaves. It makes a gentle, meditative composition
here in company with pink and white candelabra
primrose Primula pulverulenta 'Bartley', some
variegated water irises, and the still water.*

ANETHUM GRAVEOLENS Dill.
*A self-seeding annual. Every
part of the plant has a fresh,
• aromatic fragrance.*

ALCEA ROSEA
'CHATER'S DOUBLE'
Hollyhock. *A rust-free
biennial selection in
• varied colors.*

LILIUM 'LE REVE'
Lily. *An oriental lily
producing flowers with
the most heavenly
sweet scent.* •

COLOR INTERPLAY ▶
The soft contours of clipped golden yews stand as focal points in a view where the colors of columbines play off each other like gentle breezes. Above, the red-violet blossoms of a late-flowering redbud mix with cream-variegated green foliage.

◀ EXOTIC PAIR
Reminiscent of a Mediterranean hillside, sharp yellow Foeniculum vulgare *joins the violet hues of* Verbena patagonica. *When the sun is high at its midsummer peak, stronger pastels will still sing out.*

▼ SUBTLE SUGGESTION
This mix of plants has an easy, natural charm. The pink blooms of Dianthus *'Doris' echo the tones of daisy* Erigeron mucronatum. *Catmint* Nepeta *'Six Hills Giant' adds a dusky lavender glow.*

Autumn

Brilliantly tinted foliage dances along
outstretched branches of Japanese
maples, made all the more gorgeous
by glimpses of contrasting green in the
grass beneath and roughly textured,
lichened bark of adjoining trees.

PALETTE FOR AUTUMN

A month or so before the end of summer a new mood stirs, heralding autumn. Nights are cooler, heavy dews collect, and the garden's color palette begins to change. As autumn gathers pace, sultry tones take over. Oranges, reds, and golden yellows triumph in chrysanthemums and dahlias. Asters amaze in marvelous purples, blues, and mellow pinks. Then flowers give way to glowing berries and the glorious spectacle of autumn leaves.

EVENING IN THE RHYTHM OF LIFE

Decay is more apparent in wild parts of the garden. Leaves turn color and fall, providing nourishment for next year's growth: green is overtaken by gold, rust, and brown. Mists drift in these mornings, especially around water. As the sun breaks through, the garden basks again in warm and honeyed light.

• YELLOW reflects the sinking of the sun and remembered summer warmth in many daisy flowers. Later, foliage adds its mellow tones.

• PINK reigns strongly at this time of year in dusky hues, and veers toward the soft violets and blues of the color wheel. Their beauty is seen in many sedums, New England asters, and hydrangeas.

• ORANGE fits autumn to perfection: it is as if the myriad patchwork of summer color has been heaped on a fire in a burst of flame at the end of the year.

• RED is rich and deep in autumn. It is seen in many chrysanthemums and dahlias, as well as the changing leaves of sumacs, cherries, and maples, which glimmer darkly before they fall.

• SCARLET puts on a glorious show in holly, bittersweet, viburnum, and pyracantha fruits, which are some of the most vividly colored autumn berries.

INCANDESCENT FIRE

SCARLET, VERMILION, RUBY, carmine, crimson: all these violent shades are centered around vivacious red. Autumn offers a plethora of incandescent colors in various forms of dahlia, nerine, and crocosmia. In addition, a wealth of berries and other fruits add to the colorful pageant. Their range of tone is extremely forward – even brash – and all leap out of their beds in colors that astound us with their sheer audacity. Most potent against green, they also clamor with a raucous voice when intermixed with purples and blues.

ASTER NOVI-BELGII 'EVENTIDE' New York aster. *A favorite, pretty perennial with lavender daisy flowers.*

NERINE SARNIENSIS VAR. CORUSCA Guernsey lily. *A bulb. It grows outdoors only in mild places.*

RELATED COLOR SWATCH

If pure primary red is one of the most forward colors of the wheel, scarlet and reds that lean toward orange are surely the most fiery. Their jack-in-a-box capacity to spring out of the landscape can almost overwhelm, yet their lively tribute to the joy of summer's plenty is an apt prelude to the quieter, less active seasons. This grouping teams the wonderfully crystalline flowers of nerine with cotoneaster and fluffy New York asters.

*COTONEASTER HUPEHENSIS.
A deciduous shrub of arching
habit with the advantage of
yellow autumn color and
• profuse fruit clusters.*

DESIGNED TO SHOCK
Flame red and crimson dahlias with tropical-leaved cannas and purple verbena make vivacious companions. Dahlias 'Bishop of Llandaff' and 'Sure Thing' are about as spirited as any flowers can be, and look even more so in association with the verbena.

RACING THROUGH THE SEASONS
Crocosmia quickly forms clumps of its late summer to autumn flower spires in colors ranging from orange to gold and yellow to blazing red. Purple Verbena patagonica jumps up in front.

THE SETTING SUN

HARMONY SITS at the heart of autumn in the tawny rusts, rich dark reds, earth browns, and radiant burnt orange that share the hot part of the color wheel. Their closely allied warmth reflects the tones of bonfires and a setting sun, and in the garden they lend a melodious yet fading heat to the year's color parade. Beside autumnal favorites, such as the floribunda roses seen with bronze canna foliage at left, the final glory of summer goes on in begonias, fuchsias, geraniums, and nasturtiums.

SYMPATHETIC MARRIAGE

DAHLIA Water-lily type. A tuberous perennial, one of the numerous border hybrids. It will flower until first frost.

RELATED COLOR SWATCH

A dusky group lit by the candylike orange of red-hot pokers will look especially wondrous as the sun dips to the horizon. This grouping blends chocolate and gold, russet and blood red. It takes us from the sharp, crackling midst of the bonfire to its dark, smoky outer edges that barely catch the dwindling rays of daylight.

COMPOSITION FOR ONE VOICE
All the harmonious colors of the season are captured in a single plant. Shifting from glowing scarlet through dusky orange to old gold, the petals of sneezeweed Helenium autumnale *are set off by large globular pompons of hazy ochre and toasted brown.*

ENDURING MELODY
*Chrysanthemums have a pungent scent that echoes
their embered hues. These reflexed and pompon
cultivars are covered in flower for weeks from late
summer until cold weather sets in. Underplanted
below, nasturtiums ping against their vivid leaves.*

KNIPHOFIA TRIANGULARIS
Red-hot poker. A perennial
with small flower spikes borne
on stout stems.

LEYCESTERIA FORMOSA
Himalayan honeysuckle.
A deciduous shrub. The
white flowers with purple-
red bracts produce purplish
autumn fruits.

CHRYSANTHEMUM Non-
disbudded type. An early
autumn perennial bearing
sprays of flowers that are
ideal for cutting.

RADIANT GOLD

NOT ONLY CAN autumn's touch turn many plants to gleaming gold: many autumn plants bear golden flowers and fruits besides. From red-gold to pale gold and brilliant yellow-golds, this is the color that fits the mellow feeling of autumn. It's important to make the most of each season's particular gifts so that beds and borders (containers, too) can shine in every month. Autumn flowers with golden-leaved shrubs will look marvelously apt now and still appeal for the rest of the year.

RELATED COLOR SWATCH

Plants whose flowers span the change of summer to autumn are especially valuable. There are even some indefatigable annuals such as begonias, snapdragons, and marigolds, all with forms in gold, that start with an early summer flush and last to the first frost. The strawflowers and chrysanthemums here will bloom from late summer right through autumn, while the young eucalyptus foliage is often tinged with gold.

CHRYSANTHEMUM 'WENDY' Spray florists' mum. *An unreliably hardy perennial bearing reflexed flowers in early autumn.*

BEFORE THE FALL
Staghorn sumac Rhus typhina, *seen in its form 'Laciniata', which makes a small tree, has leaves that expire in a gorgeous burst of color through rich gold and oranges to striking scarlet. Hickory, beech, and sassafras also supply fine autumnal golds.*

STARRY TREASURE TROVE
The strong contrast between nearly black eyes and gilded yellow petals highlights a generous clump of coneflower Rudbeckia hirta 'Marmalade'. For an especially prolific autumn show, cut back and feed the plants after their first summer flowering.

CHRYSANTHEMUM 'YELLOW BREITNER'. An early autumn perennial. It should be grown from rooted cuttings planted in late spring.

EUCALYPTUS TORQUATA Coral gum. A slender, slightly hardy evergreen tree that will reach 25ft (8m).

HELICHRYSUM BRACTEATUM Strawflower. A branching annual that flowers from summer to early autumn.

FLICKERING EMBERS

I AM ALWAYS HAPPY to return to one of my favorite color combinations. Pink and orange make such glad companions and are especially cheerful with an injection of pale or golden green. As the season moves on and the garden is readied for winter, it is good to have planned for a farewell vision of animated color. Dahlias, nerines, belladonna lilies, and later-flowering hebes contribute plenty of pinks and oranges to the season's palette. Many roses, too, have flowers and fruits in wondrous shades of these two colors.

AMARYLLIS BELLADONNA
Belladonna lily. *A bulb producing its flower stems in early autumn after the leaves die down.*

RELATED COLOR SWATCH

Rugosa rose hips the size and color of tiny tomatoes, fragile papery ribbed lanterns of *Physalis alkekengi*, and luminous nerines provide elements of brilliant orange in this group for an autumn border. The sugar pink of sweetly fragrant belladonna lilies and rouged carmine of *Hebe* 'La Séduisante' impart a glow of soft warmth.

ROSA RUGOSA 'SCABROSA' Species hybrid. *A dense shrub. The large fruits follow a long succession of richly scented, cupped, single pink flowers.*

SPLENDID LATE ARRAY
A deep border can be every bit as delightful in autumn as it is in summer. Fringing and overflowing the lawn's edge are crocosmia, amaranth, penstemon, yarrow, rudbeckia, mallow, dahlia, and rose. All are alive with form, texture, and joyful play of color.

FIREBRAND DISPLAY
Red-hot pokers stand like gleaming torches against a bronze-purple smoke tree and deep pink Joe Pye weed. Pale lemon-green mullein and goat's beard emphasize the zingy clash of orange with pink.

HEBE 'LA SEDUISANTE'.
A barely hardy evergreen shrub for a sheltered site, with dense flower spikes • throughout autumn.

NERINE 'CORUSCA MAJOR'.
Plant this bulb in the shelter of a warm sunny wall and protect • from freezing.

PHYSALIS ALKEKENGI
Chinese lantern. *A perennial that needs to be controlled. Fruits hide inside • the lantern calyces.*

Winter

With the landscape of color at its
most somber, the pure clean beauty
of other detail comes into its own in
the outlines of trees, vigorous young
shoots, rich evergreens, and flowers
that shine like miniature jewels.

PALETTE FOR WINTER

Dominated by the brown of soil, the gray of bark, persistent green foliage, and a sprinkling of berries, winter may seem short on color interest. Yet the garden still has magic. The sharply defined bones of trees and shrubs laid bare produce intricate patterns. Evergreen forms abound in gold, copper, and silver-blue. Camellias and other shrubs grace the view with winter flowers, while crocuses and snowdrops speak sweet messages of spring.

A STUDY IN MINIMALISM

Crisp dried-up hortensia hydrangea heads have a spare beauty, intensified by flooding winter light. The plumed branches, with once-colorful bracts now coated in frost, are reduced to shades of frothy cappuccino. In the foreground at right, a brave little robin broods plumply atop a small evergreen rhododendron.

134

• GRAY-BROWN *is a bold feature of winter's scene in the form of bare soil, bark, and catkins. Dried leaves, held on hedging plants like hornbeams and beeches, or littering the ground, add a touch of textural interest.*

• WHITE *flowers dominate at this time. Viburnums and heathers (precious spots of light) gleam bright against somber foliage, and survive the chill of winter thanks to their energy-conserving size.*

• COPPER, *as tones of red and bronze, appears in the leaves of many plants such as pittosporum, leucothöe, photinia, phormium, and cordyline. Purple varieties extend this color range.*

• SILVER *and biting tones of iron green echo the cold patinas of winter. As with white, they give a brilliant sheen to dreary landscapes. Many conifers, santolinas, and artemisias have useful silver-gray winter foliage.*

• RICH EVERGREENS *have a special value at this time, providing definition for the garden and a suggestion of spring's freshness. Berries are a bonus on small trees and shrubs including holly, skimmia, and firethorn.*

WINTER CHEER

FEMALE *SKIMMIA JAPONICA*

BECAUSE OF THE AUSTERITY of the season, when red and green meet in the landscape, the contrast is even more intense than at other times of year. Berries will be the surest source of winter reds, if birds have not taken them all. When planning for them, remember that some plants, including skimmia (*left*), need a male and a female to produce their fruits. Winter shoots can make strong features, too. Willow *Salix alba* 'Britzensis' has a tracery of scarlet young stems that look particularly beautiful near water.

RELATED COLOR SWATCH

This vigorous quartet of plants has color sufficient to brighten the grayest outlook. A glowing collection of stout-hearted spiky holly, dogwood stems, fruiting ivy, and cotoneaster provides an exciting variety of color and texture in its glossy and ribbed evergreen foliage, mahogany winter shoots, and clustered scarlet berries. No less showy, the green ivy fruit ripens to coal black.

SKELETON FRAMEWORK
The whiplike shoots of 'Westonbirt', which is a selection of red-barked dogwood Cornus alba, *stand out boldly against snow-covered ground.* C. stolonifera *'Flaviramea' has lemon shoots in winter. Prune both low in spring to encourage young growth.*

ILEX AQUIFOLIUM
English holly. An evergreen tree that grows slowly and has many different forms. The fruit is especially profuse after dry summers.

NATURAL WONDERS
When the garden lacks color, other parts of the scene can fill the gap. The hard-edged blue of a winter sky is nature's own surprise. It makes an incredible backdrop to the brilliant red berries of cranberry bush Viburnum opulus *that follow its lace-cap white flowers and tinted autumn foliage.*

CORNUS ALBA Red-barked dogwood. *A deciduous shrub that has red bark in winter. C. alba 'Elegantissima' has variegated summer foliage.*

COTONEASTER 'CORNUBIA'. *A semievergreen shrub of arching habit. Clusters of white flowers in early summer are followed by copious quantities of berries.*

HEDERA HELIX English ivy. *A self-clinging evergreen climber with berries only on older treelike growth.*

ARCHITECTURAL GREEN

I T IS IN WINTER that greens come with renewed vigor into their
own, for this is the time of year when much of the competition
is gone from the garden. Bold shapes and textures (not forgetting
those of branches and bark) impress themselves on areas of sparse
color, replacing it with structural interest. Boxwood and yew clip
beautifully into topiaries; privet gives a tidy hedge. If other color
is desired, many trees have forms with gold, blue, or silver foliage.

*LARIX DECIDUA European
larch. A deciduous conifer that
has light green foliage, golden in
autumn. It grows fast, reaching
as much as 100ft (30m).* ●

RELATED COLOR SWATCH

Striking leaves and twigs in varied shades of green, as
well as excitingly different textures, produce splendid
effects. In the garden (which may languish in winter)
they make noteworthy features that transform it from
summer's poor relation into something really special.
Here are deciduous larch twigs, covered in lichen and
moss, joining New Zealand flax, crinkly pittosporum,
silver-backed elaeagnus, and sprays of golden cypress.

ORNAMENTAL FROSTING
*Mahonias, especially the taller ones, have drama in their leaves,
held like outstretched palm fronds on plants that make shrubs or
small trees. Barely hardy M. lomarifolia (my favorite) and the
hardier hybrid M. x media 'Charity' have scented flowers.*

CORSICAN BEAUTY
Lenten rose Helleborus lividus *subsp.* corsicus *often produces its pale greenish white flowers in late winter, with successive showings until spring. Its spine-toothed leaves are evergreen. For subtle color, choose H. x sternii 'Blackthorn' with its silver-pink foliage and green flowers flushed pink.*

PHORMIUM TENAX New Zealand flax. A tender perennial variegated in gold, bronze, silver, cream, and purple. •

ELAEAGNUS x *EBBINGEI. An evergreen shrub. The tiny tubular white autumn flowers have a strong gardenia scent.* •

PITTOSPORUM TENUIFOLIUM 'VARIEGATUM'. A large shrub or small evergreen tree that thrives by the sea. •

CUPRESSUS MACROCARPA 'GOLDCREST' Monterey cypress. A fast-growing evergreen conifer with • *lemon-scented foliage.*

As trees or pruned into shape, yews can live to hundreds of years old: one famous English topiary garden has yews that are now in their fiftieth decade. It's useful to remember, when planning such strongly ornamental shapes, that the plants can put on as much as 10in (25cm) a year.

◀ COAT OF MANY COLORS
You may need to search for winter hues and patterns, but they are really superb in their detail. So it is with Leucothöe fontanesiana 'Rainbow'. The evergreen leaves, shown in their seasonal red dress, are further defined by a dusting of frost.

▲ HANGING WONDERS
Silk-tassel bush Garrya elliptica *bears magnificent catkins that hang on its branches like Christmas decorations from midwinter to spring. Careful siting is a must, for its dark green foliage can make it a dull feature at other times when the flowers are gone.*

▲ YEAR-ROUND SPECTACLE
On a cold winter morning, boxwood and mounding evergreen honeysuckle Lonicera nitida *take on a blue-green frosted air. They're particularly good topiary subjects, as are privet and yew, and will look fantastic at every season, including winter.*

MIDWINTER WHITE

THE COLOR OF SNOW AND FROST seems particularly right for winter plantings and the mood of quiet watchfulness. When the weather is mild, white brings nostalgia, too, for the crisp beauty of hoarier days. The vagaries of regional climate will dictate the plants you choose. At this time of year, the absence of eye-engaging color lends grasses and seedheads, such as those of clematis (*left*), a unique appeal. For flowers, Christmas roses are the earliest white, followed by snowdrops and – in some areas – white quince and heather.

SILKY CLEMATIS SEEDHEADS

RELATED COLOR SWATCH

This seasonal planting for a bed against the shelter of a wall will flower in mild midwinter spells through to spring. *Senecio* 'Sunshine' has leaves whose soft felted undersides are echoed in cream-white Christmas rose *Helleborus niger* and heather, opening from pink buds. Flowering quince adds blossoms of spare, pure white.

SENECIO 'SUNSHINE'. *A bushy evergreen shrub with coarse yellow flowers, best kept as a foliage plant.*

AIRS AND GRACES
Pampas grass Cortaderia selloana *needs room to create so rich an effect: plants quickly form massive clumps and are invasive. The fine ivory-colored flower plumes can reach heights of 10ft (3m). They stand all winter, but should be removed in spring.*

LATE WINTER GREETS SPRING

The first snowdrops are a welcome sight, for they seem to say that spring is not far away. Of the many sorts, I think the simple common snowdrop Galanthus nivalis *is lovely with its gray-green leaves, especially carpeting the edges of woodland.*

CHAENOMELES SPECIOSA
'NIVALIS' Flowering quince.
A deciduous, thorny shrub,
excellent for training against
a sheltered sunny wall. •

HELLEBORUS NIGER
Christmas rose. A clump-
forming evergreen perennial
with winter to spring flowers.
In sheltered sites, blooms
• appear in early winter.

ERICA ERIGENA
Heather. A tall,
slightly hardy
evergreen shrub
with flowers from
early winter until
late spring. •

PROMISE OF SPRING

WITH THE INEXORABLE movement of life, winter months give way to spring, and color creeps into the garden once more. In the meantime, some plants defy the bleak mood that can slide over midwinter, bearing flowers and foliage to make you feel that spring has already come. The scent of vigorous young growth fills the air in a burst of vitality, and hearts skip a beat. Yellows, golds, warm pinks, rich creams, and foliage greens capture the colors of early spring and act like rays of sunshine on a wintry scene.

RELATED COLOR SWATCH

This combination of pink, yellow, and white, gentle and heartening against the supple bronze leucothöe leaves and dark evergreen camellia, is hard to surpass on a winter's day. Scent is a bonus that intensifies the ebullient mood, for these white viburnum and yellow witch hazel flowers smell delicious. Plant the camellia out of morning sun so that its flowers remain spotless.

LEUCOTHÖE FONTANESIANA 'RAINBOW'. An arching evergreen shrub. The bronze young leaves mature to dark green, at first splashed pink that turns to cream.

OMEN OF SPRING
Winter aconite Eranthis hyemalis *can be really early to bloom. Its spring yellow flowers emerge brightly even through snow and ice. Each single buttercup-like bloom has a ruff of green leaves. A bit temperamental, it likes dappled shade and rich moist soil.*

LATE WINTER COLOR
*The fat buds of Japanese apricot Prunus mume
'Beni-shidare' can appear as early as late winter.
In warm periods they burst open to flood the
garden with vivid color. 'Pendula' is a weeping
form, also with early flowers but of a paler pink.*

VIBURNUM x BODNANTENSE.
*An upright deciduous shrub.
Its vanilla-scented flowers
open in mild spells from late
• autumn until early spring.*

CAMELLIA JAPONICA
'TAKASAGO'. *An evergreen
shrub, a cultivar with
flowers distinguished
by their large golden
• yellow stamens.*

HAMAMELIS MOLLIS 'PALLIDA' Chinese
*witch hazel. A large deciduous shrub with
yellow autumn foliage. The winter flowers
have an intensely sweet yet delicate scent.* •

SEASONAL PLANT IDEAS

To help you select plants by color in each of the four seasons, I've put together a list (*pages 146 to 153*) that contains some unusual kinds as well as familiar and favorite ones. It is intended simply to spark ideas of your own.

The descriptions provide notes on culture and site, flowering time, and color range of flowers (or in a few cases the colors of leaves or fruit). As a rule, the plants are best in a well-drained soil, and will flower throughout their season.

SPRING

TREES, SHRUBS, & CLIMBERS

Acacia MIMOSA, WATTLE.
Fast-growing evergreen trees. Sun, frost protection. Early spring. *Bright yellow.*

Aesculus hippocastanum HORSE CHESTNUT.
Large deciduous tree. Sun or part shade. Late spring. *Creamy white with dark pink to red blotches.*

Akebia quinata.
Deciduous or semievergreen climber. Rich soil, sun or part shade. Late spring. *Dark purple.*

Amelanchier SERVICEBERRY.
Small deciduous trees. Sun or part shade. Midspring. *White.*

Arbutus MANZANITA.
Small to large evergreen trees with reddish bark. Acid soil, sun with shelter. Midspring. Red autumn fruit. *White.*

Azara.
Evergreen shrubs or small trees. Rich soil, sun or part shade with wall shelter. *Bright yellow.*

Berberis BARBERRY.
Deciduous free-flowering shrubs. Sun. Colored autumn fruit. *Yellow, orange, apricot, red.*

Camellia.
Evergreen shrubs or small trees. Acid soil, part shade with shelter. Winter to spring. *Yellow, red, pink, white.*

CORNUS FLORIDA
'CHEROKEE CHIEF'

Chaenomeles FLOWERING QUINCE.
Deciduous shrubs. Sun or part shade. *Orange, red, pink, white.*

Choisya ternata MEXICAN ORANGE.
Evergreen, aromatic shrub. Rich soil, sun or part shade. Flowers occasionally throughout year. *White.*

Clematis montana.
Deciduous climber to 30ft/10m. Alkaline soil, base in shade, shoots in sun. Profuse four-petaled flowers. *Pink, white.*

Cornus florida FLOWERING DOGWOOD.
Small deciduous tree with showy bracts. Rich soil, sun. *Pink, white.*

Cytisus canariensis BROOM.
Large evergreen shrub. Sun with shelter. Profuse flowers late winter to midsummer. *Yellow.*

Daphne.
Evergreen & deciduous shrubs, most with scented flowers. Sun with shelter (but *D. laureola* will tolerate deep shade). *Pink, white.*

Erica cinerea,
E. x darlyensis HEATHER.
Evergreen subshrubs. Moist acid soil, sun. Winter through spring. *Pink, purple, white.*

Euphorbia characias,
E. mellifera, E. myrsinites,
E. polychroma, E. rigida.
Evergreen & deciduous sub-shrubs & perennials with showy flowerheads. Sun. *Yellow, gold, lime green.*

Forsythia.
Large deciduous shrubs. Sun or part shade. Midspring before leaves emerge. *Bright yellow.*

Kerria JAPANESE KERRIA.
Large free-flowering deciduous shrubs with single or double flowers. Sun or part shade. Midspring. *Yellow.*

Magnolia denudata,
M. salicifolia, M. x
soulangeana, M. stellata.
Deciduous large shrubs or small trees. Rich soil (best acid to neutral), sun with shelter from strong cold winds. Tulip-shaped flowers are produced before leaves unfold. *Pink, purple, white.*

Malus CRABAPPLE.
Small or medium-sized deciduous trees. Rich soil, full sun. Flowers at the same time as leaves unfold. *Pink, white.*

Osmanthus.
Medium to large evergreen shrubs. Full sun with shelter from cold wind. Scented flowers late spring. *White.*

Pieris.
Large evergreen shrubs. Moist acid soil, bright site with shade. Varieties of *P. formosa* have coral, salmon, & red new leaves at same time as flowers. *White.*

Prunus CHERRY.
Small to medium deciduous trees. Full sun. Single or double flowers mid- to late spring. (*P. sargentii* produces rich autumn color.) *Pink, white.*

Rhododendron
(includes azaleas).
Evergreen & deciduous small to large shrubs. Moist acid soil, part shade with some shelter. Bears trumpet-shaped flowers in heads, mostly late spring. *Yellow, orange, red, pink, purple, white.*

PIERIS JAPONICA 'FLAMINGO'

Ribes FLOWERING CURRANT.
Medium-sized to large deciduous
shrubs. Sun or part shade. Flowers
borne in racemes early spring.
Yellow, red, pink, white.

Sophora tetraptera KOWHAI.
Large tender deciduous shrub or
small tree. Rich soil, full sun
against a wall for shelter. Clusters
of waxy pealike flowers midspring.
Golden yellow.

Spiraea x **arguta,**
S. thunbergii BRIDALWREATH.
Medium-sized deciduous shrubs.
Wreaths of tiny flowers mid- to
late spring. *White.*

Staphylea BLADDERNUT.
Large deciduous shrubs or small
trees with vanilla-scented flowers.
Moist rich soil, full sun. Late
spring. *Pink, white.*

Syringa LILAC.
Medium to large deciduous shrubs
or small trees. Rich soil, sun or
part shade. Fragrant flowers after
2–3 years' established growth.
Pink, purple, lilac, white, cream.

Viburnum plicatum
JAPANESE SNOWBALL.
Large deciduous shrub. Moist rich
soil, full sun. Flowerheads single
or double. *Pink, white.*

ANNUALS & BIENNIALS

Bellis ENGLISH DAISY.
Grow as biennials. Rich soil, sun
or part shade. Regular dead-
heading provides single & double
flowers early spring through to
summer. *Red, pink, white.*

Erysimum WALLFLOWER.
Grow as biennials. Any neutral to
alkaline soil, sun. Highly scented
flowers produced in spikes late
spring. *Yellow, orange, red, pink,
purple, cream.*

Lunaria HONESTY.
Grow as biennials. Part shade.
Sweetly fragrant flowers mid- to
late spring. Silver seedpods
autumn. *Pink, purple, white.*

Myosotis FORGET-ME-NOT.
Grow as biennials. Moist soil, sun
or shade. Most varieties with pure
blue flowers midspring to early
summer. *Range of blue.*

ERYSIMUM 'JOHN CODRINGTON'

Senecio x **hybridus** CINERARIA.
Half-hardy biennials. Soil well-
drained but not dry, sun or part
shade. Flowerheads midspring to
early summer. *Orange, red, pink,
violet, purple, blue, white.*

PERENNIALS & BULBS

Allium ORNAMENTAL ONION.
Small to large bulbs. The narrow
straplike leaves have an onion
smell when crushed. Sun. Plant
out in autumn. Flowers, borne in
umbels, appear late spring to early
summer depending on species.
Yellow, pink, purple, blue, white.

Bergenia.
Herbaceous perennials. Sun or
part shade. Leaves large, leathery,
evergreen. Flowers in heads late
winter, spring, & early summer.
Rust, pink, purple, white.

Chionodoxa
GLORY OF THE SNOW.
Small clump-forming bulbs. Sun.
Some have flowers of purest blue.
Early spring. *Pink, blue, white.*

Crocus.
Small-growing bulbs, naturalizing
in grass. Sun or part shade. Early
spring or autumn, depending on
species. *Yellow, orange, purple,
blue, white.*

Erythronium.
Tuberous perennial that prefers a
cool climate. Rich soil, part shade
or shade. Delicate bell-shaped
flowers are borne above rosettes
of leaves late spring. *Yellow, pink,
purple, white, cream.*

Fritillaria imperialis
CROWN IMPERIAL.
Large bulb. Bright part shade.
Beautiful flowers but with an
unpleasant skunky smell. *Yellow,
orange, red.*

Fritillaria meleagris
SNAKE SKIN FRITILLARY.
Medium bulbs that will naturalize
well in grass. Bright part shade.
Brown, purple, green, white.

Galanthus SNOWDROP.
Small-growing bulbs. Sun or part
shade. Bell-shaped flowers, held
on delicate stems, early spring.
White, most with green markings.

Hyacinthoides non-scriptus
ENGLISH BLUEBELL.
Large bulbs. Will naturalize in
and carpet light woodland. Moist
soil, part shade. Lightly scented
bell flowers are borne in short
spires. *Pink, blue, white.*

Hyacinthus HYACINTH.
Small to medium-growing bulbs.
Sun or part shade. Intensely
perfumed flower spikes mid- to
late spring. *Salmon, red, pink,
purple, blue, white.*

Leucojum SNOWFLAKE.
Low to medium bulbs. Well-
drained but not dry soil, sun or
part shade. *L. vernum* (small)
& *L. aestivum* (medium) have
snowdroplike flowers with green
markings. Some species flower
autumn. *White.*

Muscari GRAPE HYACINTH.
Low clump-forming bulbs. Sun or
bright shade. Strap-shaped leaves.
Flowers have sweet butter scent.
Blue, white.

HYACINTHUS 'JAN BOS'

Narcissus DAFFODIL.
Large group of low- & medium-
growing bulbs, many of which
will naturalize well in grass. Sun
or part shade. *Yellow, orange,
pink, cream, white.*

Polygonatum
SOLOMON'S SEAL.
Elegant & demure perennials.
Rich soil, part shade. Bell-shaped
flowers are borne along leafy
stems. *White edged with green.*

Primula vulgaris
ENGLISH PRIMROSE.
Low clump-forming perennials.
Moist soil, sun or part shade.
*Yellow, gold, orange, red, pink,
purple, violet, white.*

Pulmonaria LUNGWORT.
Low-growing perennials. Sun or
part shade. *Red, pink, blue, white.*

TULIPA 'GOLDEN OXFORD'

Ranunculus asiaticus.
Half-hardy perennial, growing
from a tuber. Rich moist soil, full
sun. Semidouble and double
buttercup-like flowers. *Yellow,
orange, red, pink, white.*

Scilla.
Low-growing bulbs. Moist but
well-drained soil, sun or part
shade. *Pink, blue, white.*

Symphytum COMFREY.
Herbaceous perennials that grow
fast & will naturalize freely. Sun
or shade. Flowers are bell-shaped.
Red, pink, blue, cream, white.

Tulipa TULIP.
Very large genus of bulbs. Sun or
part shade. *All except blue, often in
combinations.*

Viola PANSY & VIOLET.
Low perennials ranging from tiny
violets to larger hybrid pansies.
Moist but well-drained soil, sun
or part shade. *Yellow, gold, orange,
red, violet, purple, blue, cream.*

SUMMER

TREES, SHRUBS, & CLIMBERS

Abutilon.
Tender deciduous shrubs with bell-shaped flowers. Sun with shelter. *Yellow, orange, red, pink, lilac, white.*

Aesculus HORSE CHESTNUT.
Large deciduous trees & shrubs. Sun or part shade. Flowers in panicles. *Pink, white, cream.*

Brugmansia
ANGEL'S TRUMPETS.
Fast-growing tender deciduous & evergreen shrubs (white flowers scented.) Sun. Poisonous. *Gold, orange, apricot, pink, purple, white.*

Buddleia BUTTERFLY BUSH.
Fast-growing deciduous shrubs with flowers in panicles. Sun. *Orange, red, pink, purple, lilac, white, cream.*

Ceanothus.
Large evergreen & deciduous shrubs, sometimes small trees. Neutral or acid soil, sun. *Mostly blue, some pink & white.*

Cistus ROCK ROSE.
Evergreen shrubs. Sun, shelter. Flowers last one day. *Pink, white.*

Clematis.
Long-flowering, mostly deciduous climbers. Rich soil with roots in shade, shoots in sun. *All except orange, turquoise.*

Cotinus SMOKE TREE.
Large deciduous shrubs or small trees. Sun. *C. coggygria* 'Royal Purple' & others have purple foliage. *Fawn, gray.*

CLEMATIS VENOSA 'VIOLACEA'

CEANOTHUS ARBOREUS 'TREWITHEN BLUE'

Deutzia.
Medium deciduous shrubs. Rich soil, sun. Massed flowers early to midsummer. *Red, pink, white.*

Escallonia.
Tall half hardy evergreen shrubs, good for coastal planting. Sun. Clusters of spring flowers. *Red, pink, white.*

Eucalyptus GUM TREE.
Fast-growing evergreen trees with attractive foliage. Sun. *E. gunnii, E. pauciflora, E. perriniana* are half hardy. *Mostly silver-blue.*

Fremontodendron.
Large half hardy evergreen or semievergreen shrubs. Light soil, sun with wall shelter. Spring to late autumn. *Yellow.*

Fuchsia.
Mostly tender deciduous shrubs, ideal for containers. Rich soil, part shade. High summer to late autumn. *Orange, red, scarlet, crimson, pink, purple, lilac, white.*

Hebe.
Tender to half-hardy evergreen shrubs, grown for their flower spikes & foliage. Sun with shelter from cold winds. *Red, pink, purple, blue, white.*

Helianthemum ROCK ROSE.
Small, long-flowering evergreen shrubs. Sun. *Yellow, orange, red, pink, white.*

Heliotropium CHERRY PIE.
Tender evergreen shrubs, usually grown as annuals. Rich soil, sun. Highly scented flowers are borne in corymbs all summer until frost. *Violet, purple, white.*

Hibiscus syriacus
ROSE-OF-SHARON.
Long-flowering deciduous shrubs, small trees. Sun. Late summer. *Red, pink, purple, white.*

Hypericum ST. JOHN'S WORT.
Deciduous & evergreen shrubs. Sun or part shade. Profuse flowers late summer & autumn. *Yellow.*

Jasminum officinale, J. parkeri, J. revolutum
JASMINE.
Tender to half-hardy evergreen, semievergreen, or deciduous climbers. Best in sun. Summer to autumn. *Yellow, white.*

Kolkwitzia BEAUTY BUSH.
Large deciduous shrubs. Rich soil, sun. Midsummer. *Pink, white.*

Lantana.
Tender evergreen shrubs, usually grown as annuals, good for containers. Multicolored flower heads. Poisonous. *Yellow, orange, red, pink, lavender, white.*

Lavandula LAVENDER.
Hardy & half-hardy mounding evergreen shrubs. Sun. Mid- to late summer. *Pink, purple, lavender, white.*

Lavatera MALLOW.
Short-lived deciduous shrubs & annuals. Well-drained soil, sun. *Pale pink, white.*

Lonicera HONEYSUCKLE.
Deciduous & evergreen shrubs & climbers, most with very fragrant flowers. Sun or part shade. Some sorts flower in autumn. *Yellow, red, pink, cream.*

Olearia DAISY BUSH.
Tender evergreen shrubs, excellent for seaside planting. Sun with shelter. *O. semidentata* has mauve flowers. *White.*

Passiflora caerulea
BLUE PASSIONFLOWER.
Half-hardy, flowering climber. *White flushed pink with purple.*

Pelargonium GERANIUM.
Large group of tender subshrubs. Sun or bright shade. Many have patterned leaves. *Orange, red, pink, purple, white.*

Philadelphus MOCK ORANGE.
Mostly large deciduous shrubs. Sun. A favorite is *P.* 'Belle Etoile', with white petals marked purple at base. *P. microphyllus* & *P.* 'Sybille' are both good for smaller gardens. Most *Philadelphus* flowers are highly scented. *White.*

Phlomis JERUSALEM SAGE.
Half-hardy evergreen shrubs with aromatic gray foliage. Most species have whorled flowers. Sun. Slightly tender *P. italica* has lilac-pink flowers. *Mostly yellow.*

Phygelius.
Half-hardy evergreen or semievergreen shrubs & subshrubs, with tubular flowers. Sun. Mid- to late summer & autumn. *Yellow, orange, red.*

ROSA 'BIG PURPLE'

Plumbago LEADWORT.
Tender evergreen shrubs, usually grown as annuals, good for containers. Sun. *Blue, white.*

Potentilla CINQUEFOIL.
Long-flowering deciduous shrubs & perennials. Sun or part shade. Many cultivars are available. *Yellow, orange, red, pink, white, cream.*

Rosa ROSE.
Deciduous shrubs & climbers with variable flowers. Rich moist soil, sun. Flowers through summer & into autumn. *All except blue.*

Santolina.
Aromatic evergreen shrubs. Sun. *S. chamaecyparissus* has silver, *S. pinnata* subsp. *neapolitanum* gray foliage. *Yellow.*

Spartium junceum
SPANISH BROOM.
Deciduous, almost leafless shrub.
Light soil, sun. Scented flowers
early summer to autumn. *Yellow.*

Weigela.
Medium to large deciduous
shrubs. Moist but well-drained
soil, sun or part shade. Profuse
foxglovelike flowers early to
midsummer. *Red, pink, white.*

Wisteria.
Tall deciduous climbers with
attractively divided leaves &
sweet-scented flowers in long
racemes. Sun. *Pink, lilac, white.*

ANNUALS & BIENNIALS

Ageratum.
Low half-hardy annuals with
flowers in fluffy corymbs, good for
containers. Moist well-drained
soil, sun. *Pink, lilac, blue, white.*

Alcea HOLLYHOCK.
Biennials or perennials grown as
annuals. Rich moist, well-drained
soil, sun. Single or double flowers
grow up spikes to 15ft/3m. *Yellow,
apricot, red, pink, white.*

Antirrhinum SNAPDRAGON.
Perennials grown as annuals. Rich
soil, sun. Lightly scented flowers.
A range of heights and habits.
Yellow, orange, red, pink, white.

Arctotis x hybrida.
Usually grown as annual. Sun.
Bears a succession of large daisy
flowers, often zoned. *Yellow,
orange, red, pink, white.*

Calceolaria.
Mostly half-hardy annuals &
biennials. Rich, moist but well-
drained soil, sun. Spotted flowers
like tiny inflated balloons. *Yellow,
orange, red, pink.*

Calendula POT MARIGOLD.
Self-seeding annuals. Any not-
too-rich soil, sun. Single or double
flowers. Deadhead for flowering
through summer and autumn.
Yellow, orange, apricot, cream.

Celosia.
Annuals with plumes of flowers,
for planting out in early summer,
ideal for containers. Sun. *Yellow,
orange, red, pink, purple, cream.*

Centaurea CORNFLOWER.
Annuals & biennials. Full sun.
Some staking may be required.
Pink, purple, blue, white.

Clarkia.
Continuous-flowering annuals,
good for cutting. Sun, needs cool
weather. *Red, pink, salmon, white.*

Coleus.
Evergreen perennials grown as
annuals mostly for their foliage.
Rich soil, sun. *All colors.*

Convolvulus.
Long-flowering annuals &
perennials, mostly climbers. Sun.
Pink, purple, lilac, white.

Cosmos.
Annuals & perennials with
feathery foliage. Light soil, sun.
Yellow, orange, pink, white.

Digitalis purpurea FOXGLOVE.
Biennial with many forms. Moist
well-drained soil, part shade. Tall
spikes of spot-throated, hooded
flowers early to midsummer. *Rust,
pink, purple, white, cream.*

Echium lycopsis.
Bushy, profuse annual. Sun. Midsummer. *Blue-pink, purple, white.*

Eschscholzia californica
CALIFORNIA POPPY.
Long-flowering annual with ferny
silver foliage and poppylike
flowers. Sun. *Yellow, orange, red,
pink, white.*

Gomphrena
GLOBE AMARANTH.
Annuals with cloverlike flowers,
good for drying. Full sun. Mid- to
late summer. *Yellow, orange, red,
pink, purple, white.*

HELICHRYSUM BRACTEATUM

Helichrysum bracteatum
STRAWFLOWER.
Easily grown annual. Sun. *Large
range in all except blue, green.*

Iberis umbellata CANDYTUFT.
Low-growing annual. Sun. *Mostly
pink, lilac, lavender, some white.*

Lathyrus odoratus SWEET PEA.
Climbing annual with beautifully
scented flowers. Rich soil, sun.
*Orange, red, pink, violet, purple,
blue, white, cream.*

Linaria maroccana
TOADFLAX.
Half-hardy annual with small
spurred flowers. Light soil, sun.
Yellow, red, pink, lilac, white.

Linum FLAX.
Tiny-leaved annuals & perennials
with richly colored flowers. Sun.
Pink, red, yellow, blue.

Mathiola STOCK.
Annuals & biennials with
intensely scented flowers. Sun or
part shade. *Red, pink, purple, lilac,
white, cream.*

Nemesia.
Profuse, long-flowering annuals.
Either neutral or acid soil, sun.
Midsummer. *Yellow, orange, red,
pink, blue, white.*

Nicotiana TOBACCO PLANT.
Mostly tender perennials usually
grown as annuals. Moist, well-
drained soil, sun or part shade.
Red, pink, green, white.

Nigella LOVE-IN-A-MIST.
Annuals easily grown from seed.
Sun. Seed pods are decorative in
autumn. *Pink, blue, white.*

Petunia.
Free-flowering annuals. Do not
plant in the same soil two years
running. Sun. Flowers in purple
& blue often have good perfume.
*Red, pink, violet, purple, blue,
white, cream.*

Phacelia campanularia.
Bushy annual. Light soil, sun.
Intense blues.

Portulaca.
Mostly succulents grown as
annuals. Brilliant wide cuplike
flowers open with the sun. Light
soil, full sun. *Yellow, red, pink,
purple, white.*

Salvia splendens SAGE.
Very colorful annual with spires
of flowers, good for containers.
Sun. *Orange, apricot, scarlet, pink,
purple, mauve, white.*

Schizanthus.
Tall long-flowering annuals. The
flowers often have yellow spotted
throats. Rich soil, full sun. *Red,
pink, purple, white.*

Silene CATCHFLY.
Annuals with bright or pastel
flowers. Sun or bright shade.
Pink, lilac, white, cream.

Tagetes MARIGOLD.
Long-flowering annuals. Sun.
Deadhead regularly for best
results. *Yellow, gold, orange.*

NICOTIANA 'LIME GREEN'

Tropaeolum majus
NASTURTIUM.
Scrambling annual, also good for
containers, with many forms.
Sun. Susceptible to aphid attack.
Yellow, orange, red, white, cream.

Ursinia.
Annuals & perennials with finely
cut foliage & daisy flowers, ideal
for containers. Sun. *Yellow,
orange, red.*

Verbena x hybrida.
Annual with numerous forms,
excellent for containers including
hanging baskets. Rich soil, sun.
Red, pink, violet, purple, white.

Viola x wittrockiana PANSY.
Annual. Rich moist well-drained
soil, sun or part shade. Numerous
forms flower throughout year in
mild weather. *All except green.*

Zinnia.
Annuals with pompon flowers.
Good fertile well-drained soil &
plenty of sun. *All colors (including
lime green) except blue.*

PERENNIALS & BULBS

Aconitum MONKSHOOD. Perennials with spires of hooded flowers. Rich moist soil, part shade. All parts poisonous. *Pink, violet, blue, white.*

Alchemilla LADY'S MANTLE. Low perennials spreading rapidly. Part shade. Flower spires dry well. *Yellow-green.*

Allium ORNAMENTAL ONION. Bulbs. Many have attractive globular flowerheads. Sun. Late spring to midsummer. *Yellow, pink, purple, white.*

AQUILEGIA VULGARIS 'NIVEA'

Alstroemeria. Perennials with many hybrid forms. Established plants resent disturbance. Sun. *Yellow, orange, red, pink, purple, white.*

Anchusa azurea. Perennial with flowers in spires to 6ft/2m. Sun. *Intense blues.*

Anigozanthos KANGAROO PAW. Tender perennials. Moist acid soil, sun. *Yellow, mustard, scarlet, pink, plum, green.*

Aquilegia COLUMBINE. Medium perennials with spurred flowers, easily grown from seed. Moist well-drained soil, sun or part shade. Early summer. *Yellow, pink, purple, lilac, blue, white.*

Armeria THRIFT. Low clump-forming evergreen perennials with small globes of flowers. Well-drained soil, sun. *Red, pink, white.*

Artemisia WORMWOOD. Perennials, some evergreen or semievergreen, grown for their featherlike foliage, which is often aromatic. Sun. Remove leggy growths and prune to shape. *Silver, silver-gray.*

Astilbe. Moisture-loving perennials with feathery plumes of flowers. Damp soil, part shade. Midsummer. *Red, pink, white.*

Astrantia MASTERWORT. Medium-sized perennials with paper-thin flowers. Moist but well-drained soil, part shade. *Pink, green, white.*

Begonia. Tender perennials mostly from tubers or rhizomes, usually grown as annuals, with showy leaves & profuse flowers. Rich moist well-drained soil, part shade or shade. *Yellow, orange, red, pink, white.*

Borago BORAGE. Invasive perennials with hairy leaves & stems of lovely nodding flowers. Sun or part shade. Low-growing *B. pygmaea* is particularly attractive. *Blue, white.*

Campanula BELLFLOWER. Perennials ranging from rock plants to taller midborder sorts. Sun or part shade. *Pink, purple, blue, white, cream.*

Canna. Tall half-hardy perennials with swordlike, sometimes red, leaves. Grow in containers or plant out early summer; move indoors before frost. *Yellow, orange, scarlet, pink, cream.*

Coreopsis. Medium-sized perennials & annuals with large daisy flowers. Light soil, sun. Mid- to late summer. *Yellow, gold, orange, red.*

Crambe cordifolia KALE. Perennial with masses of small flowers held 6ft/2m above very large leaves. Alkaline soil best, sun. *White.*

Dahlia. Perennials growing from tubers with many flower forms and plant heights. Plant late spring, rich soil, sun. Water freely. Mid-to late summer. *All except blue, green.*

Delphinium. Tall perennials (most need staking) with flowers in spires. Rich soil, sun. Cut out flowering stems when finished for a second showing. Prefer cooler weather. *Pink, purple, blue, white, cream.*

Dianthus PINKS. Low & taller perennials with single or double flowers, often clove-scented. Neutral to alkaline very well-drained soil, sun. Stake taller sorts. Modern *Dianthus* have a long bloom season. *Yellow, orange, red, pink, purple, white.*

Erigeron FLEABANE. Low perennials with profuse daisy flowers over a long period. Sun. *Pink, violet, purple, lilac.*

Eryngium SEA HOLLY. Medium perennials with striking silvery foliage. Flowerheads are thistlelike and surrounded by feathery bracts. Sun. *Mostly silver-blue, some purple, green.*

Euphorbia SPURGE. Very large genus with many perennials, grown for their mounding shape and showy bracts (*E. griffithii* has red bracts). Sun. Bracts *usually lime green.*

Felicia BLUE MARGUERITE. Tender perennials often grown as annuals forming leafy hummocks. Prefers well-drained soil, sun with shelter from cold winds. Successive flowerings. *Bright blue.*

Foeniculum FENNEL. Decorative tall perennial herb with feathery foliage and flowers in umbels. Sun. *Yellow-green.*

DELPHINIUM 'FENELLA'

COREOPSIS GRANDIFLORA 'BADENGOLD'

Filipendula MEADOWSWEET. Tall perennials with flowers in panicles. Moist well-drained soil, sun or part shade. *Pink, white.*

Gaillardia. Medium perennials & annuals with dazzling daisy flowers. Sun. Throughout summer & early autumn. *Yellow, orange, red.*

Galega GOAT'S RUE. Medium perennials with spires of pealike flowers. Sun or part shade. Needs staking. Midsummer. *Pink, blue, white.*

Gazania. Low half-hardy perennials usually grown as annuals with large daisy flowers. Some have silver foliage. Full sun. *Yellow, orange, red, pink, lime green, white.*

Geranium CRANESBILL. Large genus with many low perennials. Sun or part shade. *G. cinereum, G. endressii, G. nodosum, & G. subcaulescens* are all long flowering. *Carmine, pink, violet, purple, blue, white.*

Gerbera. Low tender perennials with rosettes of leaves & showy large daisy flowers. Sun with shelter. *Yellow, orange, red, pink, white.*

Geum. Small to medium perennials with small clusters of flowers. Moist well-drained soil, sun or part shade. *Orange, red, pink.*

Gladiolus. Medium to tall corms with lily-like florets opening up tall stems. Rich soil, sun. *All except blue.*

Gypsophila BABY'S-BREATH.
Small to medium perennials with a haze of tiny flowers borne on slender branching stems. Alkaline soil, sun. *Pink, white.*

Hemerocallis DAYLILY.
Medium perennials with lilylike flowers usually borne over a long period. Rich soil, sun or part shade. *Yellow, orange, red, pink, purple, white.*

Impatiens BALSAM.
Mostly tender perennials (some annuals), mound-forming, some with decorative leaves. Excellent for containers. Moist well-drained soil in sun, part shade, or shade. All need frost protection. *Yellow, orange, red, pink, purple, white.*

Iris.
Growing from a rhizome, plants bear swordlike leaves and often fragrant flowers. Any soil, part shade, sun. *I. laevigata* and its relatives favor damp places. Most early summer (some winter or spring). *All colors.*

Kniphofia RED-HOT POKER.
Perennials with tall flower spikes. Many hybrids have silver-green swordlike leaves. Sun. Summer & autumn. *Yellow, orange, red, white, cream.*

Liatris GAYFEATHER.
Medium perennials with strap-shaped leaves. Flowers are borne in spikes. Rich light soil, sun. *Pink, purple, white.*

Lilium LILY.
Large-flowered bulbs usually with several often intensely scented blooms to a stem. Excellent for containers. Rich soil, sun or part shade. *Yellow, orange, red, purple, white, cream.*

Lobelia.
Half-hardy perennials & annuals. Rich moist well-drained soil, part shade. *L. fulgens* (barely hardy) has scarlet flowers. *Red, pink, purple, blue, white.*

Lupinus LUPINE.
Medium to tall perennials with spires of sometimes bicolored pealike flowers. Dislikes alkaline soil and hot summers. Sun or part shade. Prone to aphid attack. Cut back for second flowering. *Yellow, orange, red, pink, purple, blue.*

Lychnis CAMPION.
Small to medium perennials. Sun. *L. coronaria* has silver foliage & strikingly vivid pink flowers. *Orange, red, pink, white.*

Lysimachia LOOSESTRIFE.
Medium-sized perennials that are often invasive. Sun or part shade. *L. nummularia* 'Aurea' is a lovely creeper with flowers & foliage both yellow. *Yellow, white.*

Lythrum PURPLE LOOSESTRIFE.
Medium to tall perennials with flowers in spires. Moist soil, sun or part shade. Midsummer. *Pink.*

PAPAVER NUDICALE
'SUMMER BREEZE'

Meconopsis.
Lovely but short-lived perennials, including wonderful blue poppies *M. betonicifolia* & *M. grandis*. Rich moist but well-drained acid soil, part shade. *Yellow, orange, pink, purple, blue, white.*

Mimulus MONKEY FLOWER.
Perennials, annuals & shrubs with snapdragon-like flowers. Moist soil, sun or part shade. *Yellow, orange, red, pink, white.*

Mirabilis FOUR-O'CLOCK.
Half-hardy tuberous perennials. Small scented trumpet flowers open in the evening. Rich soil, sun. *Yellow, red, pink, white.*

Monarda didyma BEE BALM.
Medium-sized perennial with aromatic leaves and whorled flowers. Rich soil, sun. *Red, pink, purple, white.*

Nepeta CATMINT.
Low to medium wide-spreading perennials with spires of flowers over a long period. Sun or part shade. *Lavender, blue, white.*

Nymphaea WATER LILY.
Perennial water plants, many tender, with often scented star-shaped single or double flowers. Rich soil in pool or mesh container, sun or bright shade. *Yellow, red, pink, purple, white.*

Oenothera EVENING PRIMROSE.
Low to tall perennials & some annuals with poppylike flowers. Sun. *Yellow, orange, pink, white.*

Paeonia lactiflora PEONY.
Clump-forming perennial including many hybrids, with single or double flowers that are often scented. Rich moist but well-drained soil, sun or part shade. *Red, pink, cream, white.*

Papaver POPPY.
Medium perennials & annuals, many self-seeding. Sun. *Yellow, orange, red, pink, purple, white.*

Penstemon.
Low to medium perennials with foxglovelike flowers in spires. Sun. *Red, pink, purple, blue, white.*

Phlox paniculata.
Medium perennial with many forms. Scented flowers are borne in panicles. Rich moist but well-drained soil, sun. *Orange, red, pink, purple, lilac, violet, white.*

Physostegia OBEDIENT PLANT.
Medium perennials with trumpet-shaped flowers in spires. Sun or part shade. *Pink, purple, white.*

Polemonium JACOB'S LADDER.
Medium perennials with ferny foliage. Moist but well-drained soil, sun or part shade. *Blue, lavender, white.*

Polygonum SMARTWEED.
Long-flowering perennials & climbers, sometimes invasive, with flowers in spikes. Moist well-drained soil, sun or part shade. *Red, pink, white.*

Primula.
Perennials with flowers often borne in candelabra form. Moist soil (good by water), sun or part shade. *Yellow, orange, red, pink, purple, white.*

Pyrethrum.
Perennials with daisy flowers. Sun. Early summer. *Red, pink, purple, white.*

Romneya TREE POPPY.
Invasive but beautiful suckering silver-leaved perennials with large sweet-scented poppy flowers. Borderline hardy. Sun. Mid- to late summer. *White.*

Roscoea.
Low to medium tuberous perennials with orchidlike flowers. Rich moist but well-drained soil, part shade. *Yellow, purple, cream, white.*

Scabiosa caucasica SCABIOUS.
Medium perennial with frilled poppylike flowers. Sun. *Pink, violet, blue, white.*

Sidalcea CHECKERBLOOM.
Medium-sized perennials with spires of hollyhock-like flowers borne over a long period. Sun. *Red, pink, white.*

Thalictrum.
Medium to tall perennials with feathery flowers above feathered foliage. Rich moist well-drained soil, sun. *Yellow, pink, lilac, white.*

Tradescantia SPIDERWORT.
Medium hardy perennials with flowers borne over a long period. Rich moist but well-drained soil, sun or part shade. *Pink, purple, blue, white.*

Verbascum MULLEIN.
Often tall-stemmed, short-lived perennials & some annuals. Sun. *V. chaixii* & *V. olympicum* have rosettes of silver leaves. *Yellow, pink, purple, white.*

Veronica SPEEDWELL.
Small to medium perennials with flowers in spikes, often needing support. Rich moist well-drained soil, sun. *Pink, blue, white.*

PRIMULA 'IRIS MAINWARING'

AUTUMN

TREES, SHRUBS, & CLIMBERS

Acer circinatum, A. ginnala, A. japonicum, A. palmatum, A. rubrum & others MAPLE.
Small, medium, & large deciduous trees, many with vivid autumn foliage and some bearing ornamental winged fruits. Moist but well-drained soil, sun or part shade. *Brilliant yellow, gold, orange, red.*

Cotoneaster.
Medium to large deciduous & evergreen shrubs with small white summer flowers followed by colored berries. Sun. *Yellow, orange, red.*

Erica HEATHER.
Low evergreen subshrubs, many flowering through autumn. Light, moist but well-drained acid soil, sun. *E. cinerea* & *E.vagans* and their forms are recommended. *Pink, purple, white.*

ACER CIRCINATUM

Hydrangea.
Medium to large deciduous shrubs & tall deciduous or evergreen climbers with showy flowerheads. Rich soil (for blue sorts, acid), part shade. Summer to autumn, depending on the form chosen. *Red, pink, purple, blue, white.*

Liriodendron TULIP TREE.
Large deciduous trees grown for their orange and green flowers (produced only on adult plants in late spring) and autumn color. Sun or part shade. *Light gold.*

Malus coronaria 'Charlottae', M. trilobata, M. tschonoskii CRABAPPLE.
Medium deciduous trees with good autumn color. Rich soil, sun or part shade. *Brilliant gold, red, purple.*

Phygelius.
Half-hardy evergreen shrubs usually grown as hardy perennials. Flowers are trumpet shaped & borne on tall stalks. Sun with shelter. Late summer & autumn. *Yellow, orange, red.*

Pyracantha FIRETHORN.
Large spiny evergreen shrubs with hawthornlike summer flowers followed by showy berries. Sun or part shade. *Yellow, orange, red.*

Quercus coccinea, Q. rubra, & others OAK.
Stately deciduous trees with fiery foliage. Sun. *Yellow, orange, red.*

ANNUALS & BIENNIALS

Amaranthus caudatus LOVE-LIES-BLEEDING.
Annual with trailing racemes of flowers (*A. hybridus* with upright plumes is also good). Rich soil, sun. *Red, purple, green.*

Callistephus CHINA ASTER.
Low half-hardy annuals with double pompon flowers. Sun. *Yellow, red, pink, purple, white.*

Helianthus annuus SUNFLOWER.
Fast-growing annual. Sun. Late summer through autumn. *Yellow, gold, red, cream.*

PERENNIALS & BULBS

Amaryllis BELLADONNA LILY.
Bulbs producing sweet-scented flowers after the leaves. Sun with shelter. *Pink.*

Anemone hupehensis, A. x hybrida.
Small to medium perennials with sprays of poppylike flowers. Rich soil, sun or part shade. Late summer to autumn. *Pink or white.*

CYCLAMEN PSEUDIBERICUM

Aster.
Small to medium perennials with sprays of small daisylike flowers. Rich moist well-drained soil, sun. Susceptible to mildew & wilt but excellent for marvelous displays of color in autumn. *Pinks, violets, purples, blues, white.*

Chrysanthemum.
Large genus of perennials (& some annuals), many flowering in autumn. Forms are variable, from small single daisylike flowers to very large & showy blooms. Rich soil, sun. *All except blue.*

Cyclamen.
Tuberous perennials, occasionally evergreen. Sun or part shade. (Winter-, spring-, & summer-flowering sorts are also available.) *Carmine, pinks, red-purples, white.*

Dahlia.
Tubers producing small to large single and multipetaled flowers in a variety of different forms. Best planted late spring. Rich soil, sun. Lift tubers & store frost-free over winter. Late summer through autumn. *All except blue & green.*

Eupatorium BONESET.
Perennials, often tall growing. Moist but well-drained soil, sun or part shade. Late summer into autumn. *Red, pink, purple, white.*

Gentiana sino-ornata & hybrids GENTIAN.
Low perennials with trumpet flowers, excellent for troughs & pans. All need acid, very well-drained soil, sun. *Intense blues.*

Gladiolus.
Corms with tall flowering stems of lilylike florets that open from the bottom of the stem upward. Rich but very well-drained soil, sun. Lift corms & store frost-free over winter months. Late summer through autumn. *All except blue.*

Helenium.
Medium-sized perennials with sprays of daisylike flowerheads. Sun. Mid- to late summer and autumn. *Yellow, orange, red.*

Nerine.
Half-hardy bulbs with stems of trumpet-shaped flowers. Full sun against the shelter of a warm wall. *N. bowdenii* is particularly good. Most need protection from frost). *Orange, red, pink, white.*

Rudbeckia BLACK-EYED SUSAN, GLORIOSA DAISY.
Medium perennials (annuals & biennials) with daisylike flowers, excellent for cutting. Sun. *Yellow, orange, red.*

Schizostylis CRIMSON FLAG.
Perennials producing spikes of flowers like small gladioli from rhizomes. Borderline hardy. Rich soil, sun with shelter from cold winds. Mid- to late autumn. *Red, pink, white.*

Solidago GOLDENROD.
Mostly large perennials with feathery heads of flowers. Sun or part shade. Some species are very vigorous and in borders have a tendency to overcrowding. *Yellow, gold.*

DAHLIA 'HILLCREST ROYAL'

WINTER

TREES, SHRUBS, & CLIMBERS

Aucuba.
Medium to large evergreen shrubs including variegated sorts. Plants of both sexes are needed to obtain berry fruits. Part shade or shade. Foliage *green or with yellow or cream markings*. Berries *red*.

Buxus BOXWOOD.
Aromatic evergreen shrubs or small trees, ideal for hedging & topiary. Sun or part shade. Main clipping is best done in spring. *Glossy dark green.*

Camellia.
Evergreen shrubs or small trees with glossy green leaves & single or double roselike flowers (some in spring). Well drained neutral to acid soil, part shade. *Yellow, red, pink, white.*

Cedrus atlantica f. glauca & others CEDAR.
Evergreen conifers, some with silver-blue needles. Sun. *Silver-blue, green.*

Chamaecyparis
FALSE CYPRESS.
Evergreen conifers including colored forms, ranging from miniatures to large trees. Sun. *Green, gold, blue, silver.*

Chimonanthus WINTERSWEET.
Deciduous wall shrub with waxy, intensely fragrant flowers on bare stems. Rich soil, in the shelter of a sunny wall. *Yellow, cream.*

Cornus alba & forms
DOGWOOD.
Deciduous shrubs with colorful winter shoots, effective beside water. Sun. Shoots *yellow, red.*

Corylopsis WINTER HAZEL.
Medium to large deciduous shrubs with racemes of sweet-scented flowers. Acid soil, sun. Late winter & spring. *Yellow, cream.*

Cryptomeria japonica & forms.
Evergreen conifers grown for their colored winter foliage. Rich moist but well-drained acid soil, part shade. *Green, bronze.*

Cupressus CYPRESS.
Small to medium evergreen conifers with tough but feathery foliage in sprays. Sun. *Green, gold, gray-blue, silver.*

Daphne.
Deciduous & evergreen small to medium shrubs usually with intensely scented flowers. Near neutral soil, sun. Evergreens D. odora 'Aureo-marginata', D. laureola (no scent, will tolerate shade), & deciduous D. mezereum flower winter into spring (other sorts flower spring & summer). *Yellow, pink, green, white.*

SKIMMIA JAPONICA

Hamamelis WITCH HAZEL.
Small deciduous trees. The sweet-scented flowers have delicate spidery petals. Rich moist well-drained acid soil, part shade. Late winter. *Yellow, orange, red.*

Hedera IVY.
Medium to tall self-clinging evergreen climbers, some with variegated foliage (H. helix 'Tricolor' has a plum-colored winter flush). Sun or shade. *Green or with gold, cream, or silver marks.*

Ilex HOLLY.
Mostly evergreen shrubs & small to large trees (some variegated) with colorful berry fruits. Rich moist well-drained soil, sun or shade. (Deciduous I. verticillata has a profusion of red berries late autumn & early winter). Foliage *green & with yellow, white, or cream markings*. Berries *yellow, orange, red, green, white, black.*

Jasminum nudiflorum
WINTER JASMINE.
Tall hardy deciduous shrub with arching stems. Sun. *Yellow.*

Juniperus JUNIPER.
Small to medium prickly-leaved evergreen conifers with colored forms (in particular low-growing ones). Sun or part shade. *Green, gold, blue, silver.*

Laurus BAY LAUREL.
Medium, aromatic evergreen tree, good for large specimen topiaries. Rich soil, sun or part shade with shelter. Plants in pots need occasional waterings in mild winter spells. *Glossy dark green.*

Lonicera HONEYSUCKLE.
See under SUMMER listing.

Mahonia.
Evergreen shrubs with decorative spiky leaves & flowers in racemes. M. x 'Charity', M. japonica, & M. lomarifolia have flowers with scent like lily-of-the-valley. Rich moist but well-drained soil, part shade. *Yellow.*

Picea SPRUCE.
Miniature to large evergreen conifers including forms with colored foliage (P. pungens f. glauca is very silvery). Moist well-drained acid soil, sun with shelter. *Green, gold, blue, silver.*

Skimmia.
Medium evergreen shrubs. Plants of both sexes are needed to obtain flowers & berries borne together in winter (but S. japonica subsp. reevesiana is self fertile). Rich moist but well-drained soil, sun or part shade. Flowers *white opening from pink buds*. Berries *scarlet.*

Taxus baccata ENGLISH YEW.
Medium evergreen conifer, excellent for topiary & hedges, females with red fruit ('Lutea' has yellow). Sun or shade. *Dark green.*

Viburnum.
Small to large deciduous & evergreen shrubs. Rich moist but well-drained soil, sun. Deciduous V. x bodnantense (vanilla scented) & V. farreri flower on bare stems. Evergreen V. tinus flowers autumn to spring. *Pink, white.*

PERENNIALS & BULBS

Bergenia.
Low evergreen perennials with large rounded leaves. Sun or part shade. Flowers are produced in mild winter weather & through spring. *Pink, purple, white.*

Crocus.
Low bulbs, best grown in large swaths. Sun. Mid- to late winter, depending on weather (some sorts flower in autumn). *Yellow, orange, red, pink, purple, blue, white.*

Eranthis WINTER ACONITE.
Low tuber bearing buttercup-like flowers surrounded by rosettes of leaves. Moist but well-drained soil, sun. Midwinter. *Yellow.*

Galanthus SNOWDROP.
Bulbs with delicate bell-shaped flowers. Moist but well-drained soil, part shade. Depending on weather, midwinter to spring. *White with green markings.*

Helleborus CHRISTMAS ROSE, LENTEN ROSE.
Evergreen & semievergreen perennials. Rich moist but well-drained soil, part shade. H. niger from early winter; H. orientalis 'Atrorubens' & H. viridis mid- & late winter & early spring. *Pink, green, white, cream.*

Iris.
See under SUMMER listing.

GALANTHUS FOSTERI

INDEX

Page numbers that appear in **bold type** refer you to a plant featured in a "Related Color Swatch." Page numbers that appear in normal Roman type direct you to text on a plant or subject. Page numbers that appear in *italic type* direct you to a picture with a caption.

GARDEN CREDITS

Publisher's Note to Readers

Many of the gardens that were photographed by Steven Wooster for *Malcolm Hillier's Color Garden* will be found on this page; but where people have asked not to be included, their desire for anonymity has been respected and their names and the locations of their gardens do not appear. The publisher would be grateful to be told of unintended errors, omissions, or incorrectly named plants. In the credits, a letter following a page number shows picture position: t = top; b = bottom; c = center; l = left; r = right. No letter identifies a full-page picture.

• **Ayrlies Garden** (New Zealand), Bev & Malcolm McConnell 73t, 79t
• **Barnsley House,** Rosemary Verey 28bl, 112t
• **Bates Green Farmhouse,** Mr. & Mrs. J. McCulthan 102b
• **Kathy Boardman & Serena Blackie** (New Zealand) 71b
• **Bodnant Garden** 46b, 57t
• **Bourton House Garden,** Mr. & Mrs. R. Paice 86b
• **Brook Cottage,** Mr. & Mrs. D. Hodges 22t, 45t
• **The Winter Garden at The Cambridge Botanic Gardens** 34r, 132 & 133, 136b, 138b
• **The Beth Chatto Gardens** 22b, 32t, 32b, 35t, 35b, 43tr, 49b, 50bl, 53t, 60 & 61, 73b, 85t, 95t, 97t, 97b, 122b, 129t
• **Mrs. Chea** 92t
• **Chiffchaffs,** Mr. & Mrs. K.R. Potts 48bl, 59t
• **Mrs. Cooke** (New Zealand) 85bl
• **Denmans Garden,** John Brookes 31t, 31br, 46t, 68t, 115t
• **East Lambrook Manor,** Mr. & Mrs. A. Norton 52t, 81t, 119
• **Elizabeth & Roger Edmonds** (New Zealand) 74b
• **Feeringbury Manor,** Mr. & Mrs. Giles Coode Adams 42t
• **Fitz House,** Major Mordaunt-Hare 67, 84
• **Fulham Park Gardens,** Anthony Noel 92b
• **Gardens of the Mind,** Ivan Hicks 64t, 69t

• **Gethsemane Garden** (New Zealand), Bev & Ken Loader 72t, 108b
• **Great Dixter,** Christopher Lloyd 12b, 31bl, 56t, 65t, 66b, 76bl, 77, 78b, 85br, 94b, 99t, 99b, 100b, 104b,111t, 116t, 118t, 125t, 125b, 126t, 127t, 131t
• **Hadspen House,** Nori & Sandra Pope 10b, 78t, 104t, 105b
• **Hampton Court Gardens** 47tr, 50br, 51
• **Hazelby House,** Prue & Martin Lane-Fox 28t, 111b
• **The Sir Harold Hillier Gardens & Arboretum** 128
• **Isabella Plantation,** Richmond Park 48t, 55t, 56b
• **Kelberdale,** Stan & Chris Abbot 89b
• **Kennerton Priory,** The Hon. Mrs. Healing 24b, 33t, 33b, 76br
• **The Keukenhof Gardens** (Holland) 14b, 24c, 44b, 59b
• **Leonardslee Garden,** The Loder Family 58
• **Elizabeth Luisetti** (New Zealand) 116b, 118b
• **Luquis** (New Zealand) 81b
• **Matai Moana,** Daphne & Hugh Wilson 37t, 80, 87t, 107t
• **The Mien Rhys Gardens** (Holland) 68b, 71t, 103t
• **Milton Lodge,** Mr. D.C. Tudway Quilter 87t
• **Nymans Garden** 108b
• **Ohinetahi** (New Zealand), John & Pauline Trengrove 93, 105t, 112b
• **Owl Cottage** Mrs. A.L. Hutchinson 72b

• **Putsborough Manor,** Mr. & Mrs. T.W. Bigge 76t
• **Saling Hall,** Hugh & Judy Johnson 16b, 40b, 42b
• **St. Paul's Walden Bury** Simon Bowes Lyon 18b
• **Sticky Wicket,** Peter & Pam Lewis 88, 89t
• **Kitty & Victor Sunde** (New Zealand) 106b, 109
• **Titoki Point** (New Zealand), Gordon & Annette Collier 66t, 82t, 90b, 114, 115b, 117t
• **Turn Ends** 38 & 39
• **Waimarino** (New Zealand), Liz & Rod Morrow 75t
• **Westonbirt Arboretum** 120 & 121
• **White Windows,** Mr. & Mrs. B. Sterndale Bonnett 91t
• **Wilsons Mill** (New Zealand), Mr. & Mrs. Izard 101t, 159
• **Winterhome Garden** (New Zealand), Susan & Richard McFarlane 83t

ACKNOWLEDGMENTS

Author's Acknowledgments

First, and most important, I would like to thank my business partner Quentin Roake, who has shared, advised, and encouraged throughout the production of *Color Garden* with his keen intelligence and valued critical objectivity. Special thanks also to the two photographers, Steven Wooster, who has captured in all the outdoor location pictures (including those in the section on color theory) the colors and moods of the seasons with such inspired clarity; and Stephen Hayward, whose studio shots for the section on color theory, as well as the four seasonal plant palettes and thirty plant color swatches, form a stunning addition to the book. Finally, I would like to thank friends at the Richmond Office of Dorling Kindersley, in particular project editor Gillian Roberts and art editor Debbie Myatt, who are together so inspirational a team, and who help to make all our work into such a happy experience.

Publisher's Acknowledgments

Thanks to Hilary Bird for the index; Mark Bracey for computer support; Caroline Church for the line artworks; Barbara Ellis for checking the text; Elaine Hewson for design assistance; Isobel Holland and Bella Pringle for editorial assistance; and Mel Roberts for being a devoted and exacting editorial guardian angel.

The Commissioned Photographs

Studio photographs and the location picture on page 140 *(bottom right)* by Stephen Hayward. Outdoor location pictures by Steven Wooster. Plant portraits for Seasonal Plant Ideas as follows: Andy Butler (146 *left*, 148 *top*, 150 *right*); Clive Boursnell (148 *left*, *right*); Eric Crichton (151 *right*); Howard Rice (152 *left*); Neil Fletcher (147 *center* and *right*, 149 *right*, 151 *center*, 152 *right*); Andrew Lawson (147 *left*, 150 *left*); and Steven Wooster (146 *right*, 149 *left*, 150 *center*, 152 *center*, 153 *left* and *right*).

OTHER PICTURE CAPTIONS
Outdoor location pictures on pages 1 and 4 are described in "Random Planting" (p. 73) and "Daring Display" (p. 108). Those on pages 2, 5, 159, and 160 are described below.

ENTICING PATHWAY
Woodsy shade welcomes the wanderer and beckons onward into the cool darkness. Filtering through, sun sheds its playful summer light over pink, yellow, and a host of lowly greens.

ZESTFUL CONTRAST
Against lime green euphorbia bracts, a single glorious pink tulip looks almost edible. Sharp greens in foliage or flowers give a huge boost to almost every other color in the garden.

HAPPY DAYS
A tumult of gentle country colors leads lupines, catmint, roses, Jerusalem sage, and foxgloves into a joyous disarray of purples and pinks, highlighted by primrose yellow and white.

SUNNY SIDE OF THE HEDGE
An ancient wild pear stands gaunt, looming over the bastion of a great yew hedge. Its gray bark is warmed and soothed by shafts of brilliant autumn sun and the azure sky.